DNA of a Champion Salesperson

P Raghuraman
Tanmay Dubey

Invincible Publishers

First Printing: 2019

ISBN: 978-93-89600-13-1

Invincible Publishers

Registered Address: 201A, SAS Tower, Sector 38, Gurgaon - 122003

We dedicate this in two parts. First part is to all the sales persons in the world who continue to work towards achieving their targets despite all the pressures they face. They keep the world moving and the GDP growing. Second part is to our families for being always there and supporting us unconditionally in all our endeavors. We know that you don't give us any targets. But we assure you, we are going to achieve them.

*Acknowledgement*

I graduated as a Mechanical Engineer and almost unplanned I landed into the world of IT Sales. After having spent 20 fruitful years doing Sales in Fortune 500 companies like HP, Oracle and DELL, I was wanting to share the tips and mantras that made me successful. During my days with HP, Raghuraman was my senior and I worked very closely with him. He inspired me in so many ways and I always looked up to him whenever I found myself staring at a possible black hole in my sales profession. Recently, during a *chai pe charcha* he expressed a similar desire to write a book which will have all the gyan, learnings and experiences that is squeezed in one place ready to be enjoyed with. And there we are….. *DNA of a Champion Sales Person*….is a book that is very close to my heart. I have collected valuable experiences from my life as a sales person and filtered them into this book drop by drop. I would be eternally thankful to Raghuraman for giving me an opportunity to be part of this project and a big SHOUT OUT to the young and energetic team of Invincible publishers under the dynamic leadership of Ajay Setia without whom the project would not have seen the light of the day.

\- **Tanmay Dubey**

After my engineering, I started my career in a cement factory running around coal mills, cement mills, Kiln and the machinery. I always had this feeling of "something remaining unfulfilled" as I would return to my quarters every day. 15 months later, on a train journey, as I was returning back to the factory after a brief vacation, I met this gentleman, called KC (that's how we call him till date). We got talking and over the evening I opened out to him. After listening me he said, why don't you try sales? I was completely taken aback and not sure I will make it in sales profession. He encouraged me and gave me opportunity to become a sales rep in his Hyderabad branch, where he was the Branch head of a Computer Brand, subject to my clearing interviews with his top bosses. Well I snatched the opportunity, cleared both the interviews (with the National Head and the CEO) and in the month of January 1993 started hitting the streets as a sales person. It has been more than 25 years now and I have not looked back. At this juncture I want to thank all my managers, mentors and colleagues from whom I learnt a lot and I continue to learn till date....From being a successful front end sales person, to being even more successful product manager, to running large businesses and managing large and talented teams, I grew from strength to strength. My journey has taken me through many legendary and large companies like Redington, Acer, AMD, HP etc. Today I run my own sales training company and have trained and honed thousands of sales persons to realise their strengths, identify areas of improvement and work on becoming Champion Sales Persons. In the course of this journey is when I met my talented co-author, Tanmay Dubey, who not only is a trained sales person but who can transform words from verbal to written in a manner that reader will find easy to comprehend. The learning we have put together in this book is in essence what we have learnt from many great sales people and from our own successes and failures. If there is one myth that we want to burst through this book is the popular belief by many people that you need to be a “born salesman” to be in sales profession. The reality is, “Sales People are not born, they are made”! With grooming from your bosses, attending on-line and face to face trainings regularly and with help from practically relevant book like this one that you are holding in your hand, you can become a Champion Sales Person. Tell yourself, “I have the DNAs of a Champion Sales Person and I will be super successful in my sales career”.

- **P Raghuraman**

Table of Contents

Glossary

- **Account** - An account in Management parlance is any specific end customer. It can be an organization or firm.
- **Account Manager** - An **account manager** maintains the company's existing relationships with a client or group of clients so that they will continue dealing with the company for business.
- **Agency** - a business or organization providing a particular service on behalf of another company, person, or group
- **Competition** - a person or people or an organization over whom one is attempting to establish one's supremacy or superiority; the opposition.
- **Commit** - a pledge or bind made to senior management, on the revenue or volume that you will achieve against your sales targets.
- **Channel** - a method or a system for communication or distribution of products and services
- **Dealer** - a person who buys and sells goods
- **Distributor** - an agent who buys in bulk from brand/ manufacturer and supplies goods to retailers or dealers in smaller quantities.
- **Product Mix** - the complete range of products offered by a company.

- **Product Positioning** - is the process marketers use to determine how to best communicate their **products**' attributes to their target customers based on customer needs, competitive pressures, available communication channels and carefully crafted key messages.
- **Purchase Order** - is a commercial document with legal validity and is the final document issued by a buyer to a seller indicating types, quantities, and agreed prices for products or services. Once the seller accepts the purchase order, he needs to supply the items mentioned in the purchase order. Both the seller and the buyer need to adhere to fulfill the terms and conditions mentioned in the purchase order.
- **Quarter** - Four equal or corresponding parts into which the financial year is divided. A typical financial year has four quarters. April-May-June, July-August-September, October-November-December and January-February-March.
- **Sales Call** - Meeting taken by a sales person with an existing or prospective customer, generally at customer premises.

Preface

Sales is an art, and everyone performs it!

Most of you would probably recall instances from your school or college days when the class teacher asked everyone in the class what was their aim in life or what does each student want to be in life. You would have heard, with happiness and a lot of zest, many of your classmates sharing the kind of professions they would want to pursue in life. Being a Doctor or an Engineer scored way higher than being a Writer, Painter, Dancer, Actor, Astronaut, Police, Army. Did you hear anyone saying "I want to be a Sales Person."

Even if some brave kid would have said that for sure the kid would have given enough reason to the class to giggle and risk being ridiculed for choosing to be a 'Sales Person'. Our bet is, no kid would have even thought of "sales" as a profession.

To choose "sales" or to be a "sales person" is often treated a derogatory profession, almost like witchcraft in our society. Many a times, people choose sales, if they don't get any other job. It is perceived as a tough profession which drags you into a lifestyle of being extremely busy, full of pressure, chasing numbers, facing rejection time and again, not sure of how much money you take home, no job security and yet maintaining a fake smile come what may in front of your customers. However,when we look around, a Doctor is trying to sell his services to clients. A Hospital proclaiming itself to be the best in the world, an Engineer who has designed a state of the art machine or a developer who has developed a piece of technology, all of them are striving hard to sell it. An actor, writer, dancer, all of them cannot live a successful life without wearing a sales cap.

Why, even a finance person, admin person or an HR person try hard and sell themselves internally to their bosses by talking about their achievement, in the hope of getting a promotion or salary increment. You have to *sell* yourself to grow professionally in every career.

It is for precisely the reasons stated above we decided to demystify the perceptions that are wrongly held in people's mind and wanted to tell the world that Sales is both an *Art and Science*, it can be learned and the skill set can be developed by anyone scientifically, using a step by step process that we have mentioned in this book.

This book is primarily for four types of people:

1. **Salespeople** who have just started their career and have less than one year experience. This book will help them do the right things from the early stages of their career so that they can achieve success quickly and grow faster, professionally.
2. **Experienced Salespeople** with many years of work experience, who want to get back to basics and reinvent their career and also to get their careers back on the growth trajectory
3. **Sales Managers,** Business owners and other sales leaders, who want to train their team members on professional selling skills and shape them up to become productive contributors.
4. **Students** completing their Management or other

Professional graduation programs who want to get into a sales career.

So, go ahead and embrace the life-changing principles that are mentioned in the following pages, for your life is not going to be the same once you start applying them in your daily life.

A word of advice at this point! This book is not for casual reading. We encourage you to play with the book, write on the pages, take ACTION! Practice the exercises given at the end of each chapter. Remember, while practice makes a man perfect, it makes a Sales Person not just excellent but also wealthier! You will start realizing the gains only when you start practicing the principles.

All the best !!

Happy Reading and Happy Selling!

P Raghuraman and Tanmay Dubey

SALES STORY 1

The time before taking off is hard

It's been more than three hours since Rajat was waiting outside the IT Manager, Mr Rao's cabin, biting his fingernails. Sometimes (*of late many times*) Rajat who was a Mechanical Engineer wondered whether he did the right thing by chucking his factory engineer job to take up a career in IT Sales.

The field of Information Technology (IT) as they say is fastest-growing, and anyone and almost everyone doing anything related to IT was growing or was destined to grow fast. On the face of it, the decision of making this career transition looked reasonable. But, it has been close to three months since he made the career shift and became a sales executive with the Bangalore branch of a big computer manufacturing company and he was not able to close a single sale till date!

Zilch. Nada. Nil. Zero. Need to check out in a dictionary to see if there are other words to signify "nothing", he said to himself. Bemused at his situation.

"Did I do hara-kiri with my career" Rajat wondered.

He shook up suddenly, realizing that the words came out aloud. Embarrassed, he looked at his sides and realized he was alone in the waiting area. Most of the employees at the customer's office have left for the day. Rajat looked up at his watch. *6.30PM.* His gaze went outside the window. The twilight was looking darker to him. Many questions of self-doubt sprinted across his mind.

Where am I going wrong? Am I not prospecting well and building a good sales funnel? Am I messing up on my customer relationships? Many of my prospects do seem to like me. Is my product knowledge so bad? Is my pitch bad? Why is none of my sales commitments materializing? '*My boss is kind to me. He is giving me time to settle but for how long!*' He said to himself.

He dreaded the day when after a string of repeated failures, he would be called by his Boss and would be sacked.

"I don't have reasons to fight back also! I have been getting enough time to prove myself, and I have not shown any result." Such occasional emotional outbursts shook Rajat's self-motivation time and again.

Rajat's manager had accompanied him for a few customer meetings to see if he can help him move forward on his deals. This was one such case where Rajat has been following with the prospect regularly for two months, last week he had requested his boss to accompany him for an important meeting to handle objections raised by the prospect, regarding the solution quoted by Rajat and about their company. Subsequently, the prospect had told them that they would call for a final meeting in a week. The call came in today.

Unfortunately, his boss was not in town. Initially, he felt shaky taking the meeting alone, but on second thought, his pride did not allow him to call any other senior colleague to accompany him for that closure meeting. After all, he might be new to IT sales, but he had spent considerable time knowing the customer and developing a relationship that he could bank on himself to close the deal.

"Today is my day. I am not going to let it be anything different. I will not leave the customer's office without the Purchase Order in my hand" was the thought that had bought him here. His chain of thoughts was broken when, Mr Rao, the IT Manager who had kept him waiting came out of his cabin and said "Rajat, come on in! Sorry for keeping you waiting."

*"Now or never"*Rajat muttered to himself, with heartbeat beating as loud as a drum, he picked up his bag and walked inside Mr Rao's cabin. To negotiate the deal.

Mulling Exercise:

1. *What did you observe about Rajat's state of Mind?*
2. *Why Couldn't He sell for three months?*
3. *Was he under full control to drive closure and win the deal? Did he close the deal?*

******

DNA Number 1: CONFIDENT: HAVING THE WILL TO WIN

Sales Person without confidence is like a sports person out of form and physically unfit. We see how, many talented players, whom everyone thought are going to make it big, have ended their career with a whimper.

Do successful salespeople have three hands, four legs and two brains? NO, they are people just like Rajat, but people with ABSOLUTE CONFIDENCE.

What is confidence? Pick one from the three answers below:

1. *It is something readily available that you can just buy it off the shelf.*
2. *It is something you can learn from your colleagues and seniors.*
3. *It is something you have to build yourself.*

Yes, the answer is 3. Confidence is something you have to build yourself.

You need to continually tell yourself – "If I cannot do it, nobody can."

Remember that you are the captain of your ship, and nobody can guide your ship, i.e.Your sales career, better than yourself.

How does a salesperson become confident? Choose the right answer:

1. By always telling yourself, "*I can do it. If I cannot make it happen, nobody can.*"
2. By being thorough on product knowledge. Knowing completely about the products, services and solutions that you are selling.

3. Being able to articulate the benefits that customer can enjoy from buying your product and the PROBLEM that your PRODUCT SOLVES for them.
4. Keeping yourself updated on the latest developments around the product category that you are selling, the industry you are in and your competition.
5. By being well prepared for the sales meeting, especially on handling whatever objections the customer throws at you.
6. All of the above.

Well, the answer is 6. You need ALL the above to be confident.

******

How does one acquire confidence?

To acquire confidence, you need the 3Ps.

The first P – Product Knowledge–How thorough is your knowledge of the products you sell.

- You should know in DETAIL about the product or service or solution that you are selling.
- You should be able to talk about all the FEATURES that you charge for.
- You must be able to prove or demonstrate the ADVANTAGES, i.e. You should be able to show how each of the features you talk about delivers performance in real life.
- You should be able to articulate the BENEFITS accrued to the customer.
- Last but not the least when you do all the above you should be able to RELATE to the Customer's BIG PROBLEM that your product would solve and make their life more comfortable and productive.

Following the above steps, you will see how *self belief* will start trickling into you. You will be able to

- Answer any question about your product, company, services, policies and competition to customer's satisfaction.
- Showcase and prove to the customer how your product or service makes their lives better

The second P – Preparation–How prepared are you before going for a sales call

Do you know, Research says that only 20% to 30% of sales meetings are productive, and the opportunity moves to the next stage in the sales cycle. A whopping 70% to 80% meetings end up in failures. By failure we mean, the deal never materializes. You never get that business. The reason is simple. You are not prepared for the meeting with the customer.

Have you ever heard of Sachin Tendulkar or Roger Federer skipping practice sessions regularly? How many times you have heard of a live concert of A R Rahman or Michael Jackson being termed mediocre? Chances are "Never". Despite their Himalayan achievements, they practice and prepare every day and keep themselves ready to deliver anytime.

They keep their tools sharp at all times.

Whereas for an average salesperson, out of the ten calls he takes, eight turns out to be ordinary, leading to frustration and losing confidence.

Here is P.O.L.K.A technique to be well prepared for your sales meetings:

1. **P**ractice your sales pitch before going out for a call.
2. **O**rganize all the equipment, collateral and supporting documents you would need for the call.

3. List out an agenda for the meeting and ensure you cover all the points of the agenda during your meeting.
4. Know answers to all possible objections that customer would throw up at you so that you can counter them effectively.
5. Always reach before time and collect your thoughts and compose yourself before the meeting starts.

Be Prepared. Keep your tools sharp at all times.

Third and most important P – Power of positive thinking–Do you sincerely believe that you will win the deal?

What is POSITIVE THINKING for a salesperson?

POSITIVE THOUGHTS

→ lead to

POSITIVE FEELINGS

→ lead to

POSITIVE BELIEFS

→ lead to

PROACTIVE ACTIONS

→ forms

DESTINY

Thinking that the customer likes you, your company and your proposal. Handling customer meetings with an optimistic mindset. When you approach the customer with a positive mindset – your sales pitch will be enthusiastic, you will try and understand the customer better, you will propose the right solution. Your interactions will be positively contagious, and almost like magic, you will find the customer responding positively.

Similarly, when you project the opportunity with optimism inside your organization, the chances of getting all the internal support and help to win the deal increase dramatically.

You have to be a **CAT** to become a positive person:

How to be a CAT :

Consciously help and add value to people you are interacting with.

Assume that people you are communicating with like you and want to help you.

Transparent in sharing necessary information and feedback.

It is a simple matter of following the 3Ps and see the increase in number of sales calls, turning out to be fruitful. Remember, CONFIDENCE is the 1st and foremost of the 10 DNAs of a Champion Sales Person. You can only be confident if you have the 3Ps

CONFIDENT CHAMPION SALESPERSON	**PRODUCT KNOWLEDGE**(*knowing in and out of what you are selling*) + **PREPARATION**(*rehearses the sales pitch to perfection and prepares for the sales call*) + **POSITIVE THINKING**(*approaching every task with optimism*)

Now let's go back to the episode of Rajat. Many of you are wondering did Rajat close the deal? Yes, Rajat closed the deal and went on to have a successful career. It is just that he took a long time to establish himself. His failures in the first couple of months pushed him to be better prepared for this customer, improve his product knowledge and start thinking positively. He was lucky to have an understanding boss who could help him. Imagine if you do not have that fortune and you are expected to deliver results from day one. Don't wait to fail and learn. Follow the 3Ps from day one and become Confident.

Make sure you imbibe the 1st DNA of a Champion Sales Person.

Be confident; Have the will to win.

DNA 1 – Ready Reckoner – 3Ps of a Confident Sales Person

CONFIDENT SALES PERSON	**PRODUCT KNOWLEDGE**(*knowing in and out of what you are selling*) + **PREPARATION**(*rehearses the sales pitch to perfection and prepares for the sales call*) + **POSITIVE THINKING**(*approaching every task with optimism*)

DNA 1 – Ready Reckoner – P.O.L.K.A technique to be well prepared for sales meetings

1. **P**ractice your sales pitch before going out for a call.
2. **O**rganize all the equipment, collateral and supporting documents you would need for the call.
3. **L**ist out an agenda for the meeting and ensure you cover all the points in the agenda during your meeting.
4. **K**now answers to all possible objections that customer would throw up at you so that you can counter them effectively.
5. **A**lways reach before time and collect your thoughts and compose yourself before the meeting starts.

DNA 1 – Ready Reckoner – Becoming a Positive Thinking CAT

Consciously help and add value to people you are interacting with.

Assume that people you are communicating with like you and want to help you.

Transparent in sharing necessary information and feedback.

DNA 1 –Self Exercise for Mr./Ms.____________________

Please write down in the box below:

What are the areas I should improve to become more confident

Never give up, for that is just the place and time that the tide will turn....

(American abolitionist and author.)
- Harriet Beecher Stowe

Notes

SALES STORY 2

Amar, Akbar, Anthony

This is the third month of the quarter, and there are just two weeks left to deliver the revenue commits. The Regional Manager is reviewing final commit numbers with his sales team.

Conversation between The Regional Manager and his salesperson, Amar -

"Boss, this deal of 100 units for Model A would be closed for sure by month end, and customer needs the delivery of material immediately, and it is exigent that we turn around the delivery," Amar said enthusiastically to his Manager

"How sure are you of the closure of this deal," His Manager asked in a stern voice. "I am 100% sure boss, I met the purchase manager, and he has confirmed that he will release the work order immediately," Amar said. After a brief pause, the manager replied, "OK Amar, basis your commitment, I am going ahead and requesting the Product Manager for a pre-build and keeping inventory ready." "That would be great Boss" Amar replied excitedly."But please don't surprise me with some last-minute issue. Remember we cannot carry inventory into next quarter. We have to bill it out by 30th of the month."

"Boss, don't worry. This will happen for sure."

Conversation between The Regional Manager and his salesperson, Akbar-

"Sir, this deal of 100 units for Model B looks very doubtful. The key decision maker is travelling, and I am not sure they will decide by month end" Akbar said timidly

"Akbar! How can you miss the sales target again? Your Sale performance is below average. If this deal doesn't happen, how are you going to do your numbers?

"Sir, I have a major challenge. I am not sure my numbers will happen…but…."

Conversation between Regional Manager and his salesperson, Anthony –

What is this list in your hand, Anthony, the Manager, asked?

"Boss, these are the list of deals that I am closing by date, by model. I will surely get these orders logged as per my commits. I have also mentioned which of the deals I need your support and what kind of support – whether it is Price or Delivery or help in resolving a service issue. I have also mentioned clients where I need you to come with me for the meetings. Please help support as per the same" Anthony said confidently. "OK, Anthony, let's discuss this list of yours in detail" replied the manager and started discussing line item by line item.

Mulling Exercise:

1. *What is the difference in attitudes of Amar, Akbar and Anthony you observe??*
2. *Who out of the three managed to do whatever they had committed?*
3. *Why is commitment important for a salesperson*
4. *What is the impact of a salesperson's commitment on his or her manager*

DNA Number 2: HONORS COMMITMENTS: "SAY WHAT YOU DO AND DO WHAT YOU SAY"

Commitment is defined by the Cambridge Dictionary as "***a willingness to give your time and energy to something that you believe in, or a promise or firm decision to do something.***"

To be professionally successful in a sales career, meeting your commitments is very important. People do not grow or get promoted in organizations if they continuously falter on their sales commitments. Just as in personal life, we don't tolerate people not meeting commitments, or for being unreasonable in their demands, even organizations do not tolerate salespersons who don't stick to their commitments.

Salespersons should always commit to an outcome and make it happen, except in situations beyond their control. This is what builds their credibility and helps them scale in their career to roles with increased responsibilities.

"But why is sales commitment so important? If a customer has to give business, they will give. If they don't they won't". We have often encountered such reasoning from many sales guys we work with.We will tell you why honouring a commitment is so important.

Sales is all about promising something and ensuring that promise is kept. It is about committing an outcome and ensuring that outcome is delivered. These outcomes can be an essential aspect of the sales cycle. It could be:

1. Committing on revenue and volumes that you are targeted to achieve
2. Committing on sending a detailed proposal to the customer within a specific time frame
3. Committing on closing a deal
4. Committing timely payment collection

5. Committing to your manager about fixing an appointment with the decision maker
6. Committing to customers on quality, delivery, service levels etc.
7. Forecasting the material that you want pre-built by your factory even before receipt of customer order.

Each of these commitments have an impact on other people and their commitments. In turn, it has further impact on an organization's growth, health and brand reputation.

Let's give you a few examples and explain:

1. **Committing on sales numbers** – volume and/or revenues.

<table>
<tr><td>Sales person 1's commitment
+
Sales person 2's commitment
+
Sales person 3's commitment</td><td>= Sales Manager 1's Commitment</td><td rowspan="2">=Sales Head's Commitment</td><td rowspan="2">=CEO's Commitment to Board of Directors</td></tr>
<tr><td>Sales person 4's commitment
+
Sales person 5's commitment
+
Sales person 6's commitment</td><td>=Sales Manager 2's Commitment</td></tr>
</table>

As you can see – even if one person goes back on his commitment, the entire chain gets affected.

This has an impact on critical financial parameters like

- Material forecasting and inventory management
- Factory operations
- Operating expenses – salaries, incentives etc.
- Profit & Loss statement of the business
- Marketing Expenses planned for the company

2. **Committing on deliverables to customers** – Deliveries, Service level Agreements (SLAs), Quality etc.

Suppose company's delivery period is 4 weeks and a salesperson gives aggressive commit of 3 weeks to the customer to close the deal and later the company is not able to deliver in 3 weeks, what will happen?

- You have an unhappy customer who may resort to delaying payments
- Customer may cancel the order, and the company will be stuck with material and have to bear the costs of holding it till it finds a new customer
- The salesperson loses his credibility both in front of the customer and within his organization
- The word spreads around that this brand is unreliable
- Competition use this opportunity to sell to this customer

Let's go back to the discussion on honouring number commitment, as this is the most important commitment for any salesperson.

Sales is all about committing a number, say for example 100, and ensuring you deliver not lower than 95 and at the same time not higher than 105. Plus, or Minus 5 is the only leeway the Champions take. The committed sales number is collated by the managers which are in turn shared with their managers and ultimately to senior leadership which allow them to take a lot of strategic decisions related to the critical health of the company.

If a salesperson commits 100 and delivers less than 95, that means he or she did not foresee the issues in business and take adequate precautionary actions. Similarly, if a salesperson commits 100 and delivers more than 105, that means he or she has no clue where his or her business is coming from, or he or she is a sandbagger hiding information from the management. A Champion salesperson is the one who says what he or she does and does what he or she says. Remember the Salman Khan dialogue from the film **Wanted**, *"Ekbaar jo maine commitment kar di, uske baad to mai khud ki bhi nahi suntaa" (Once I make a commitment, I don't even listen to my own excuses).*

Now, Let's go back to the sales story of Amar, Akbar and Anthony.

Amar's order did not materialize that month end. The purchase manager who had promised the purchase order had gone on leave, of which Amar was not aware of. The company was stuck with finished goods inventory of 100 units of Model A which they had to carry over to next quarter. Not only did Amar miss on his commitments, but his manager had to cut a sorry face with the management team and the factory for taking away valuable resources and not converting it into much needed revenue for the quarter. On the other hand, Akbar got his order for 100 units of Model B., but since he did not commit clearly, the company was not able to convert the order into revenue that quarter. Again, a loss of opportunity for his manager and the company.

On one side is inventory that cannot be billed for lack of customer order and on the other hand, is an order that cannot be billed due to lack of prior information. Both Amar and

Akbar are salespersons who either do not commit or do not deliver on their commitments.

And coming to Anthony, he ensured he fulfilled whatever he had committed. Organizations rate people like Anthony higher, as they deliver what they commit, and they do it consistently. *Is there a method to this madness? Can there be a framework for a manager to ensure that the numbers that is committed to him by the team are sacrosanct. Yes, there is a way!* **THE BSQ**

An accomplished CEO once devised something called *BSQ facto*r to ensure the commitments made by each salesperson was calibrated to ensure he is aware of the exact figure at which the company will exit the month or quarter.

By analyzing the commits versus actuals of each of the salespersons over some time, each salesperson was assigned a BSQ factor. The salespersons were not aware of this fact. This was strictly between the CEO and his Analyst.

Whenever the respective sales person committed a number, that number would be multiplied by his or her BSQ factor to arrive at exact commit.

Example 1: Amar always over commits and under delivers. He only delivers 80% of his commits. So his BSQ would be 0.8

Example 2: Akbar always under commits and over delivers. He delivers 150% of his commits. So his BSQ would be 1.5

Example 3: Anthony always delivers what he commits. He delivers 100% of his commits. So his BSQ would be 1.0

Come to think of it, BSQ is really an interesting and pioneering concept in sales management. Only those with BSQ equal to or close to 1 can be considered Champion Sales Persons.

For every defaulter like Amar, you have a sandbagger like Akbar. The cumulative average BSQs of the Amar, Akbar and Anthony would be that of their Regional Manager's.

By the way, BSQ stands for – Bull Shit Quotient.

What happens when you make a commitment, and you run into an obstacle?

Use the **J.U.M.P technique** to handle such a situation and overcome the obstacle. Let us elaborate this **J.U.M.P technique** :

1. **JIG-SAW PUZZLE APPROACH**: Solve it quickly yourself by making sense of the obstacle. Break down your challenge or barrier into smaller logical parts and try to see if you can make sense of each part so that they can all be put together to arrive at the complete picture.
2. **UPWARD DELEGATION**: If you are not able to handle it yourself, escalate to your superiors and ask for their help in solving the issue, by highlighting the fact that your commit is at stake if this obstacle is not removed. This will reflect well on the clarity of your thought and your commitment towards you*r comm*it.
3. **MODIFY COMMITS**: If it is an obstacle which cannot be removed due to reasons beyond your or your manager's control, then revise your commit. Yes, be upfront on this. Do not hide the fact that you are going to miss your numbers and give a nasty surprise to your managers, end of the week, month or quarter.
4. **PLAN B:** Activate your PLAN-B. This may be ambitious and only may have an outside chance of covering up for your plan A ; still, you have to try it out. With support from key stakeholders, you may be able to pull it off and ensure your original commits are still met. We are living in an age of hyper communications, and you must

ensure you are always communicating and keeping all stakeholders on the same page.

Remember – Always try to be part of the solution and not be part of the problem. When you approach your superior with a problem, also try to suggest solutions for the same and the support required for the solution.

Now going back to the story of Amar, Akbar and Anthony, *who do you think will get promoted as Manager in future when the role opens? Will it be Amar, who over commits and under delivers or Akbar, who under commits and over delivers, or, will it be Anthony, who delivers whatever he commits in a predictable manner without any shocks or surprises to the management.*

Well! No prizes for guessing. It will be Anthony! Anthony is the real Champion Sales Person. He truly adheres to the second DNA of a Champion Sales Person,

HONORS COMMITMENTS: "SAY WHAT YOU DO AND DO WHAT YOU SAY"

"I appreciate your commitment to safety, but this might be overkill for a data architect."

*****

DNA 2–Ready Reckoner - J.U.M.P Technique to overcome obstacles that may prevent you from meeting your commitments.

1. **JIG-SAW PUZZLE APPROACH**
2. **UPWARD DELEGATION**
3. **MODIFY COMMITS**
4. **PLAN B**

*****

DNA 2 – Self Exercise for Mr./Ms________________

Please write down in the box below:

What are the different types of commitments that a sales person has to make internally (within his or her organization) and externally (with customers). Write down as many as you can think:

DNA 2 – Self Exercise for Mr./Ms__________________

Please use the JIGSAW puzzle method to break down an obstacle that you face and how you will overcome that obstacle. Choose one of the three obstacles given below:

Obstacle 1: *It is just three days to month end, and the customer who had promised the Purchase Order to you is not answering your phone calls*

Obstacle 2: *The standard delivery period of your company is 2 to 3 weeks, and you are already on March 10th. You need to pick up the order, give it to your supply chain and get it invoiced and delivered to your customer by March 31st. Your customer has given a verbal go ahead and says it will take at the least 10 days to get a formal PO out of their ERP system.*

Obstacle 3: *The person with whom you are in touch within the customer organization is saying that the final decision is stuck at the top level.*

Excellence is to do a common thing in an uncommon way....

- Booker T Washington

Notes

SALES STORY 3:

What's in a plan?

Arjun and Abhishek are two "media marketing" salespersons in a newspaper company selling "advertising space". They are on a monthly target cycle and both report to the same manager. Both are smart, well educated, articulate and knowledgeable. They always leave positive impression on the people who meet them. Both carry similar kind of targets.

While Arjun consistently delivers on his numbers, Abhishek defaults at the last minute once every third or fourth month. Most of the times the issues are beyond Abhishek's control, like – The decision maker becomes ill at the crucial juncture, the weather is so bad that Abhishek is not able to travel to close the deal, there is overdue payment from a large client and hence the finance is not giving approval for the advert release, etc.

Unlike the earlier Manager, who had a lot of empathy for Abhishek, the new manager wants to understand the issue, better, so that he can help Abhishek improve on his ability to deliver on his commits. He decides to carefully analyze the working style of Abhishek over a period of time to understand him better.

Mulling Exercise:

1. *Why is Abhishek faltering on his numbers every now and then?*
2. *How is Arjun able to do it?*
3. *What happens when your boss changes and you get a new boss?*

*****

"It's a new time management app. When you click the icon, your calendar disappears!"

DNA Number 3: RIGOR IN EXECUTION–HAS A PLAN AND A BACK-UP PLAN

As Robert Burns once wisely wrote, "the best laid plans of mice and men often go astray"…

No matter how well you plan something, always expect the unexpected. In other words, just because you think you've done all you can for something to go right, things can still get messed up. One should always have a Plan B and if feasible, a Plan C.

Does this sound contradictory to DNA #1, which asks you to be positive and be confident? Well it is not. Remember two important things in sales:

1.Just like how you are well prepared and sure, there are also competitors who are going to be as well prepared, if not better prepared.

2.Secondly, not all situations are in your control. There are many things happening which are beyond your control, like

- Discounting offered by competition in the same market
- The supply/delivery or material availability in your company (*ability to fulfil demand*)
- Unforeseen medical emergencies with decision makers etc.
- Forex rate fluctuations
- Sudden change in Government policies
- Change in duties and taxes
- Weather related issues (Fog, Heavy Rains etc.)
- Social unrests like "Sudden Strikes by Government or Airline staff" and "Protests" etc.

You can give all the reasons in the world for not achieving your numbers, with the reality being that, you would be the one to get penalized on your salary or incentives for underachievement. Remember, "Success has many fathers, while failure is an Orphan"

So, it is always essential to have a back-up plan. How does one develop a plan B? The best analogy we can give is – about money.

There are three kinds of people:

First, are the people who are always hard up for money and survive on loans from friends or managing with their credit cards juggling around their payments with minimum due etc. These people are still living "hand to mouth" and managing one day at a time.

Second, there are people who have all their money in savings/checking account, who earn no interest or if they do invest, they put it in high risk investments like stock market or real estate. These people swing violently between having lot of money in hand to no money, plus, future cash flow is always a suspect.

Finally, some people ensure they keep adequate money in a savings account, have a long term fixed deposit with assured returns, have a monthly recurring deposit, have a monthly SIP based mutual fund running, or buy a "ready to move in property" etc. These are people who have money in hand all the times and are better prepared for facing any eventuality.

What is the connection to salespeople here? Just like the example above, there are three kinds of salespeople too!

First is a salesperson who is always struggling to meet his or her numbers not knowing where the next deal will come from and whether they will even meet their targets. They are always unsure and have no plan.

Second is a salesperson who is either doing more than what he commits are less than what he undertakes. Their commitments swing like a yo-yo.

Third is a salesperson in absolute control of their numbers and always deliver what they commit.

It is important is to be like the **third type**.

It is very important to learn how to prepare for eventualities to ensure you never miss your targets.To understand this better, lets return to our Sales Story of Arjun and Abhishek. After a month of observation and daily reviews, the Manager's analysis threw up the following:

	Arjun	**Abhishek**
No of sales calls made in a day	5 to 6	3 to 4
No of sales calls related to current month targets	3 to 4 per day	2 to 3 per day
No of sales calls related to business that would close only next month or next quarter	2 to 3 per day	1 at best
Size of funnel/ pipeline concerning the target	5X (5 times the target)	3X (3 times the target)
Dependence on the number of current month's deals to close to achieve the target	33%, i.e. 1 in 3 deals must close to achieve the month target	50% i.e. 1 in 2 deals must close to complete the month target

Who do you think has better chance of achieving his targets not only for the current month but also for future months? Well, let's face it. It is Arjun, who has more choice of deals to close, has a more significant funnel/pipeline to fall back on. Because he put in a **plan** in the place and went after it **piece by piece**. The sales target which looked huge at the beginning of the sales cycle started looking small and achievable over a defined period.

How does planning help

Planning helps you put an order to the activities that you intend to do. It helps you prepare as to how will you approach and eventually conduct each of the different activities that will take you to your desired goal. These activities can be

- *Making sales calls–* to an entirely new customer or a follow-up call to an existing customer or just a courtesy call.
- Preparing for and attending review meetings
- Making proposals and submitting them on time to customers
- Making travel arrangements, submitting expense claims on time etc.
- Many other things including few personal tasks that you would need to accomplish

Key elements of planning

- List down **all** the activities
- Categorize them as *Urgent vs Not-Urgent.* Urgent are those activities where there are clear deadlines
- Further, categorize them as *Important vs Not-Important.* This will help you prioritize. Prioritizing the activities will help you identify between the productive and non-productive ones. Important activities are those that help

you get close to your goals even though they may not be urgent.

Remember–not all activities that we do are directly proportional to our productivity. Many times we indulge in so called urgent activities like clearing emails, WhatsApp messages, attending to every single telephone call and keep ourselves busy 24x7. However end of the day, we are left disappointed that we didn't get the desired results.

We are not advocating you not to reply to emails, WhatsApp messages and respond to calls. What we are saying is, *learn to prioritize* the activities by setting up a fixed time in the day to respond to emails like may be every 2 hrs or so. Also, use WhatsApp for communicating to customers rather than spending 30 minutes during working hours on reading silly jokes or watching funny videos. Setup a 'free' time to go through the jokes Similarly setting up time to respond to calls can work wonders and will give you enough time in the day to execute the plan that you have created. Once you learn to prioritize you will realize most of the emails and messages are nothing more than mental farts and are not worth your time !

Remember this,

Business ≠ Busy + Ness

However,

Plan = Prioritize = Success

There are three lessons here for a salesperson

1.Plan your day better. You have to find time in your day to make sales calls that have an impact on future business along with "here and now business." Squeeze in that extra sales call. Making as many sales calls as "humanly possible" is the "first secret" of a Champion Sales Person. If you are living in a city that is plagued by traffic issues, maximize your calls by visiting more prospects in a particular area. Similarly, If you are a telesales representative, you need to figure a way to make more phone calls.

2.Building your funnel/pipeline is a never-ending activity. Make sure you have a comfortable funnel/pipeline size in relation to your target. The bigger the size of (realistic) funnel the better are your chances of consistently hitting your targets

3.Have back-up plans – If not Customer A, go to Customer B. If not Product A, sell Product B. If not Solution A, find Solution B. Explore all options legally and ethically feasible before giving up.

Having a back-up plan is not rocket science. It is all about following a strict regimen and disciplined execution. You build your back-up plan over a while, little by little. But once you get into the rigor, it becomes a "virtuous cycle."We are sharing a few steps to prepare an Invincible Sales Plan.

DNA 3–Ready Reckoner – Planning Tools and Techniques

The Invincible Sales Plan Pyramid ®

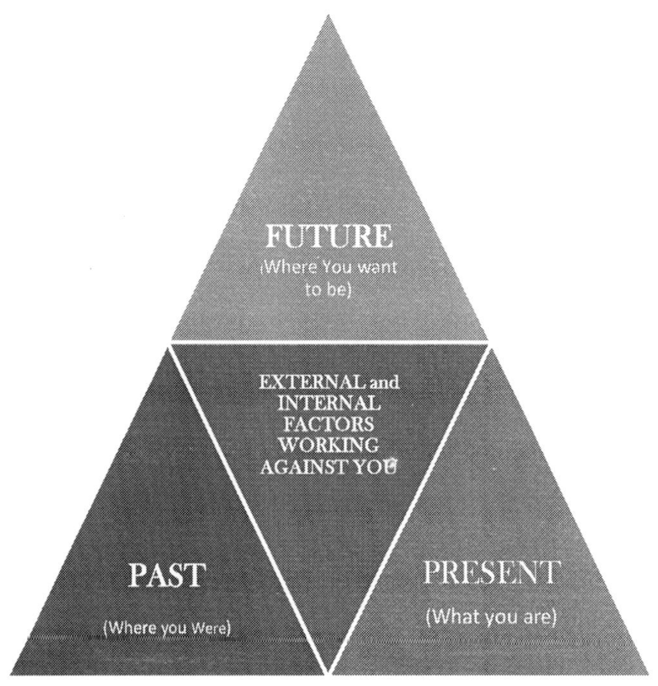

A pyramid is the most robust and balanced structure in nature

- Future lies in the top of the pyramid (aspirational goal)
- There will be many internal and external factors that will always keep pressurizing from all the sides to unbalance you.
- Past is what you can take lessons from
- The present is what you can leverage

Let get further into the brick and mortar of this pyramid and analyse from "Sales" point of view:-

Step 1 – Know your past (Where you were)

Past–Data Points Required (Sales History)
Past Revenue, Volume and Growth Data - What was your revenue, volume and growth achievement for the last one or two or three years (by month or by a quarter – depending on your sales cycle) - What was your actual performance against assigned target
Customers and Segments Data - Who are your vital existing customers who contribute to the majority of your business - In case you are handling large customers who split the business between multiple vendors, what is your share of wallet - Which industry/segment they are from, which geography or area they are from
Products and Services Data - What were the leading products, solutions and services that contributed to the majority of your past performance - What was your average selling price - Whether you are selling at higher price than your competition or at a lower price or same price
Customer Feedback - What are your customers and dealers telling about your company, products, services etc?

Present–Data Points Required (Situation on ground)
Market Trends - What are the new trends in the market? - Are customer behaviors changing? - Is there any new government policy or laws that are influencing your customers to buy more?
Competition Information - Who are your key competitors? - What are their revenues, volumes and growth numbers? - What are their strengths and weaknesses? - Are they planning anything new?
Products and Services Data - What are your current main products, solutions and services that you will be selling for the next few months/quarters - Are they meeting what customer wants? - Are they competitive? Are there any gaps?

Future–Data Points Required (Where you want to go)
<u>Target Setting</u> - Set targets for revenue, volume and growths - Ensure these targets are aligned to the growth plan of the company - Break down the targets by product, by customers, by dealers as required (depending upon the nature of your role)
<u>Action Planning</u> - To achieve the above targets, what all actions will you take - How many existing customers you will cover? - How many new customers will you add? - How many calls will you do per day?
<u>Support Required</u> - Do you need better pricing? - Are there product gaps that you want to highlight to your managers? - Are there service issues you have that need to be fixed? - What other help and support you need from your bosses?

*****

DNA 3–Ready Reckoner – Time Management Tool

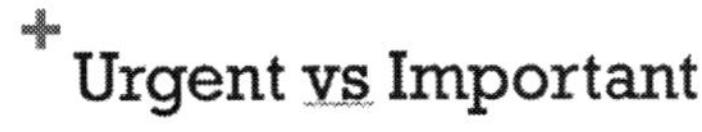

	URGENT	NOT URGENT
IMPORTANT	ACTIVITIES: Crisis Firefighting Deadlines Pressing Problems	ACTIVITIES: Prevention Relationship Building Data Analysis New Opportunities Family Time
NOT IMPORTANT	ACTIVITIES: Interruptions Some Phone Calls Some Emails Some Meetings	ACTIVITIES: Time pass Some Phone Calls Some Emails Time Wasters Pleasure activities

Activity Priority Order for effective Time Management:

1. First focus on activity which is both Urgent and Important
2. Secondly, focus on activity which is Not Urgent but Important
3. Thirdly focus on activity which is Urgent and Not Important
4. Finally comes the activities which are neither Urgent nor Important

*****

DNA 3–Self Exercise for Mr./Ms____________________

Please fill the time management tool below for each day for six days to know how much time you spend on which activity. **Use the first three columns to record the time when you started the activity.The name of the activity, and the actual time required to complete the activity. For each activity, check off the corresponding category.** This will help you to understand where your time is getting wasted and help you to identify the areas of improvement:

Time Management Tool- Daily Activity Log Chart

Date:-

Time	Activity	Time Used (In Minutes)	Email	Meetings	Telephone Calls	Planning Activity	Others (Travel/ Paper Work)

The clock is running. Make the most of today. Time waits for no man. Yesterday is history, Tomorrow is a mystery. Today is a gift. That's why it is called the present.....

- Alice Morse Earle

*****

Notes

SALES STORY 4.1

Who comes first, you or me?

Ajay broke into a competition customer with a landmark win of ₹ 70 Lakh ($100K) deal from **Customer A**. As soon as customer confirmed about the contract, Ajay called his manager Arnab and informed him about this great news. In a smart move, he also sent a text message to his manager's boss (*to impress his big boss and to ensure that he knows who has actually closed the deal!*) about the win.Soon there were congratulatory messages all around for Ajay. There was a deluge of Emails and WhatsApp messages from colleagues from all across the organization. However, Ajay was going slow in processing the paperwork and executing the deal, because he was comfortable on his targets for that month and wanted to push out this deal to next month so that his next month would also be comfortable.

But as luck would have it, Ajay got a rude jolt when he came to know from a channel partner about a deal of similar size (₹ 70Lakh) that they have lost to their competition from Customer B. The shocking part was that **Customer B** was one of his existing customers. It was a deal that both Ajay and his boss, Arnab, had taken for granted in their month's forecast. Even in his wildest imagination he never thought that he would lose this customer.

Worried about the adverse impact, this news would have for him, within his organization, Ajay hushed up the entire matter. A week later, his manager came to know about this loss from the channel partner during one of his market visits. The manager was shocked and furious that the company has lost a loyal customer!

Ajay immediately tried to douse the fire, "Boss! Don't worry. We will get the customer back. You know the customer was very unhappy with our warranty support and frequent failure of our products. In parallel, the competition gave a crazy discount which I refused as it would set a wrong precedent. Also, the new purchase manager had an unethical understanding with the competition dealer. I am sure they will not be able to execute subsequent deals, and the customer would surely come back to us.."

Arnab was unhappy that Ajay didn't tell him about this loss earlier. During the next review with his managers, he escalated about product quality issues and deteriorating post-sales service of the company, when enquired about this loss.

Mulling Exercise:

1. *Was Ajay right in hiding the loss from his manager?*
2. *What was the real reason for the deal loss?*
3. *Did his manager behave correctly after knowing about the loss?*

*****

SALES STORY 4.2

Team Player

Bharat worked at the Pune branch of a mid-sized company. He, along with his six sales colleagues, reported to the Regional Manager. This particular quarter the cumulative revenue target that the branch was supposed to deliver was ₹ 700 Lakh ($1M), and after collating all the committed deals and their respective revenue from the entire team the Regional Manager was falling short from his quarterly target by ₹ 50 Lakh. The shortfall was mainly coming from two of Bharat's colleagues who were having a rough quarter and were struggling to close their respective deals. They were exepecting to end up at 75% of their targets.

Bharat was already at 125% of his target, and anything beyond it would not give him additional incentives. He had a deal in hand for ₹ 50 lakhs which was closable within the quarter. Bharat had two options in front of him:

1. Close the deal and bail the branch and his boss out
2. Push the deal to the next quarter as it would be a tough quarter, and this would help him remain a performer next quarter also. In addition, there is no additional incentive Bharat would earn by closing the deal this quarter itself and taking his achievement to 175%.

Mulling Exercise:

1. *What should Bharat do?*
2. *Is Bharat's manager right in expecting Bharat to pitch in to fill other people's gaps*

*****

DNA Number 4: OWNERSHIP OF FAILURE–NO EGO, NO BUCK PASSING, A TEAM PLAYER

Success has many fathers but failure is an orphan!

Most people are eager to own success, but shy away from owning up failures. This is true of many sales people.

Good news is like the beautiful fragrance of an incense stick. Once it is lit, it spreads its aroma around, without having to take the stick around. Bad news is like Rotten Fruit. However much you try to hide it, the smell of the decay will spread around.

Even if you do not publicize your "good news" sooner or later, people will come to know that you were the person behind it. The "credit may be delayed" but cannot be denied. However, if you hide bad news as Ajay did in Sales Story 4.1 and your managers learn about it from other sources, you will lose your credibility. How will you face bigger failures and challenges in future?

Remember, Failures are the stepping stones to success. Own your failure immediately. You may face "short term heat", but in the long term, you are better off.

Don't let your 'I' or ego hold you back from admitting your failure. The same ego that prompts a person to broadcast his "wins" far and wide does not deem fit to convey the news of a loss.

Buck passing game!

Next issue is the case of "buck passing." Once Ajay or Arnab were confronted with their failure in holding on to an existing customer, their immediate reaction was to blame it on other team members and departments. They forgot that they are part of the same company ultimately and need to work together instead of laying blame at other people.

Neither Ajay nor his manager will qualify to become a Champion Sales Person.

Take what will happen in this case. If their "Service department" prove that customer had no service related issues and that the sales team is raising a "bogey" where there is none, Arnab and Ajay will lose face. If the product teams prove that, there was no product quality and failure issues, this will further erode Arnab and Ajay's credibility.

TEAM – Together Everybody Achieves More

How many times you have seen a sports person sacrifice his individual pursuit to ensure team wins. As cricket lovers, how many times we have seen during slog overs, new batsmen sacrificing their regular game for the sake of team and end up compromising their individual achievements and statistics.

Let's take the case of Bharat now. What should he do? Should he be a team player, or should he only think about himself? Should he ensure his branch and his manager meet their numbers or should he take care of his next quarter business?

Well, what happened was – Bharat took the additional deals to his Manager and let him decide on the same. He asked the Manager and the higher-ups to decide whether they are willing to live with a shortfall this quarter or they would like to pull in the additional businesses brought in by Bharat for next quarter, to this quarter itself.

One thing is for sure, management's impression on Bharat skyrocketed significantly. His maturity and balanced thought process impressed all his seniors.

Bharat is:

- a "Key Team Player"
- Future manager and a leader

- Champion Sales Person

Remember, the Champion would always do the following:

1. Would still be a team player and ensure whatever it takes to make the team successful. If the team wins, you also win. No point in you scoring runs and goals, while your team loses the match.
2. Will not blame colleagues for his failures. Will take complete ownership.
3. Will be the first to escalate a piece of bad news and ask for help, rather than hide issues.
4. Will be graceful in giving credit to others for his success and make the team feel proud.
5. Will always keep the company's interest in mind.

Rewards always come to Team Players:

1. Though your records, achievements and statistics may have got affected, the management and decision makers never forget your valuable role. Only team players get promoted.
2. Only a team player will become a good manager and build a great team with similar characteristics.
3. Only a team player enjoys with his team's success and shares its failures.

*****

"It appears that you're just not a team player...'

DNA 4–Self Exercise for Mr./Ms____________________

Please jot down in the box below the below two things:

1. Have you ever hid your failures from important people. Write down about the failures that you have hidden from key people and what happened after that.
2. What are the capabilities that make you a good team player?
3. What are the areas you need to improve to become a good team player?

> *"Failure is simply the opportunity to begin again, this time more intelligently"*
> ***- Henry Ford***

*****

Notes

SALES STORY 5:

Winner of a War not only looks ahead but all around

Rajan was an account manager with a large computer company called “H computers”.One of his Key Accounts was a large software solutions company called “C Software” who have been buying thousands of laptops from their competition brand, “I computers”. Rajan was tasked with mapping this account and somehow make a breakthrough.

Previously the account was handled by Arjun who could not make any breakthrough win despite managing and quoting in that account for more than six months. Arjun was meeting the IT Manager and the Purchase Manager regularly and could not get the desired breakthrough at all. Once the account got transferred to Rajan, Arjun introduced him to the IT Manager and the Purchase Manager to formally hand over the account relationship.

Rajan started meeting the customer and realized that the account was a hard nut to crack. IT manager was the one who always front ended with vendors. The Procurement manager only came at the later stage when the technical evaluation of the product was done by the IT manager. The IT manager would ask for a quote from “H Computers” but would come back saying

"Management has decided to go with "I computers."

When Rajan or his colleagues would seek a meeting with the "Management" to understand what made them go with the competition, the IT Manager would always "dilly-dally" and ensured that the meeting never happened.

Mulling Exercise:

1. *Should "H Computers" stop wasting their time with this customer?*
2. *Where was Arjun going wrong in his handling of this customer?*
3. *What should Rajan do differently to break into this account?*
4. *What is "I Computers" doing right to keep this customer in their control?*

*****

DNA Number 5: MAPS CUSTOMER THOROUGHLY – HAS A CLEAR RELATIONSHIP STRATEGY

From Gatekeeper to the CEO

OK, here is an exercise for all salespersons.

Take a client (preferably large potential client), where you have been losing business or just not able to make any headway.

Client Name: ________________________________

____

Step 1: Write down the names of all the employees from client side that you have been meeting or supposed to meet and their designations.

Names of Key People	Designation

Client Name: ________________________________

____

Step 2: Now write down their buying role in the third column. Use the abbreviated codes as given below for filling the buying role column: (Ex. If the person is a Decision Maker, mention "D" in the column)

Decision Maker – D

Approver – A

Evaluator – E

Influencer – I

Do not Know – N

Names of Key People	Designation	Buying Role

Client Name: ______________________________

____

Step 3: Write down how frequently have you met each one of them in the fourth column. Use the abbreviated codes as given below for filling the "Number of times met" column. (Ex. If the person has been met just once, mention "1" in the column)

Met more than three times – 3

Met couple of times – 2

Met once – 1

Have never met–0

Names of Key People	Designa-tion	Buying Role	Number of times met

Client Name: ______________________________

____

Step 4: Write down what according to you is this person's relationship status with you in the fifth column. Use the abbreviated codes as given below for filling the "Relationship Status" column. (*Ex. If the person likes you and your brand, mention "RS4" in the column*)

Likes me and my brand – RS4

Likes me but not my brand – RS3

Likes my brand but not me – RS2

Not Sure whether he likes me or my brand –RS1

Names of Key People	**Desig-nation**	**Buy-ing Role**	**Num-ber of times met**	**Rela-tionship Status**

Lets now take the example of "C Software" and fill this template from Arjun's perspective:

Client Name: C Software India Private Limited

Opportunity size: 200 Lacs per annum

Names of Key People	Designation	Buying Role	Number of times met	Relationship Status
Rajat Kakkar	CEO	A	0	RS1
Rajiv Sharma	CFO	A	0	RS1
Vishal Sikka	CIO	A,D	1	RS1
Ajit Ninan	COO	A,D	1	RS1
John Sebastian	Procurement Manager	E, I	3	RS2
Arumugam	IT Manager	E	3	RS3
Anil Kumar	VP-Sales	N	0	RS1
Bharat Shah	Sr. Mgr	N	0	RS1

What does this tell you?

The relationship formula for Vishal Sikka – the CIO and the boss of the IT manager who is being met regularly by Arjun is – A,D,1,RS1

He is an Approver and a Decision Maker. But he has been met just once, and Arjun is not sure if Vishal likes "H Computers" and "Arjun"

What is the action plan now for Rajan?

- He has to change "Number of times met" for Vishal from "1" to "2" and hopefully in future to "3."
- To do this, he has to take his senior managers along frequently.
- He has to ensure, by handling the discussions in those meetings properly, change Relationship status from RS1 to RS2 or RS3.
- He needs to know what are the roles of The VP-Sales and Sr. Mgr in this purchase process.

Similarly, there is an action plan for every person in this Relationship chart.

Only when you start doing the above exercise, you may realize one or more of the following:

- You hardly know more than two or three people inside the client organization.
- You don't even know the exact designation and the hierarchical positions of these persons in the organization.
- You are not sure whether the person you meet is a Decision Maker or an approver or an influencer or an evaluator.
- You are not even meeting the decision maker.
- You are not meeting the influencer.
- You have by-passed an important person.
- You are probably meeting a person who has no role to play at all.
- You are not sure if the person you are meeting is working against you or supporting you or doesn't care.
- You have met the key people only once or twice over the last few months.

- You have not met any of them enough number of times, or you have been meeting someone too many times and some others you have not met at all.
- You have not leveraged your superiors to break the ice with decision makers and approvers.
- Do you know of someone who knows the decision maker or influencer and can help you connect?
- Do you know this organization well at all?

Knowing the customer inside-out

Knowing the customer inside out is the biggest strength of a salesperson, especially in B2B space. When it comes to handling large clients, a salesperson can only be successful if he or she knows how to map a client end to end and build relationships in the unlikeliest of the places.

Few examples of how relationship strategy across various client employees can help a salesperson:

- The junior clerk at the Purchase Head's office will tell you if he saw the competition brand representatives hold extended meetings with the boss!
- A peon in a government office would know, who met whom and when!
- The finance manager would tip you off about how the MD feels your brand is too expensive. This would allow you to either work your rates or position a different product.
- One of the committee members would privately inform you that a senior manager in the purchase committee has raised a concern about your company and if you are serious about the business, you must somehow map that senior manager and address his issue.

- The Secretary to CEO would informally tell you about a meeting that is happening between the Vice President of your competition and the CEO. It should immediately raise your antenna and allow you to push for an appointment for your top management to meet up with the client CEO.
- There could be an external consultant involved who is the evaluator of the solutions proposed by different vendors. This consultant needs to be mapped, met and convinced about your solution.
- The procurement manager would be more comfortable talking about pricing and discounts to your channel partner than yourself directly.

Do not underestimate the importance of mapping as many people as possible in a prospective client's organization. And it will hold you in good stead and create an entry barrier for your competition.

Coming back to the sales story…….

After a few meetings, Rajan realized that the IT manager and the Purchase managers are evaluators only and not the influencers, decision makers or approvers. He concluded that the IT manager was not a supporter of"H" computers. Also he came to the conclusion that the Purchase Manager did not care about which vendor they were buying from as long as they got the best price and terms, and the IT manager owns responsibility for product quality and performance.

He decided to confront the purchase manager directly and ask him for help. Purchase Manager shared with him the actual issue, a perspective which was completely missing before to "H" computers.

This company had a senior leadership team which met regularly and took vital strategic decisions and the directions to take for various issues. The VP-Sales, who had a large team of customerfacing company representatives, was very clear that they would only use laptops made by "I" Computers because, as per him, the laptops were rugged, reliable and offers excellent uptime so that his sales team was always productive.

The second issue was with the CEO himself. The "I Computers" enterprise solutions team, worked with "C Software" to sell their solutions (software + hardware) together in substantial sales opportunities. So, for the CEO, the relationship with "I Computers" was not merely that of a vendor or a supplier, but that of a strategic partner who was also helping them get business for their company by offering complete solution to the market.

What did Rajan do once he learnt it?

1. He got his own CEO office to fix an appointment directly with the CEO of "C Software". They could not refuse the meeting.
2. In that meeting,Rajan ensured, his CEO, Product Head and Enterprise Solutions Sales head were present.
3. The "H Computers" CEO promised to work together in deals with "C Software" where possible and promised to have an alliance manager to work on the "selling relationship".
4. The "C Software" CEO asked them to keep in touch with their VP-Sales to take the relationship forward. (This would allow Rajan to meet the VP-Sales later)
5. The "H Computers" CEO also requested the "C Software" CEO to consider "H Computers" for their internal requirement of laptops, at least a small quantity to start with.
6. The "H Computers" product head offered two free

samples of their top end business laptop, which he requested the CEO to give it to their sales team and technical teams and ask them to use it extensively for two to three weeks and give feedback about the usage.

7. The "C Software" CEO asked Rajan to coordinate with the IT department for the same.
8. Rajan ensured in the subsequent week, the delivery and proper deployment of the demo laptops. This time he had access to even the VP of sales, whom he met for the first time.
9. They found the laptops to be of similar quality and performance as that of their existing brand.
10. Rajan got his product head to work out a special price (significantly lower than the competition) so that "C Software" now had a compelling value proposition in terms of cost savings without compromising on performance and quality.
11. Finally "C Software" placed order with "H Computers" for the first time ever.
12. In the next one year, Rajan sold close to 500 laptops at this account and achieved stellar revenues.

Moral of the story is

- It is important, to understand the customer buying process and map every single person involved in the buying process.
- When you map the customer thoroughly, you will get an opening somewhere, which you can then leverage.
- Leverage your supporters and take their help to deepen your relationship in the account
- Try and work with "do not care" employees and get as much information as possible.

- Give compelling value propositions to your non-supporters to help them change their mind.

*****

DNA 5–Ready Reckoner – Relationship Charting Tool

Client Name: ____________________________________

____

Names of Key People	Designation	Buying Role	Number of times met	Relationship Status

Abbreviations:

Buying Role	Abbreviation
Approver	A
Decision Maker	D
Evaluator	E
Influencer	I
Do not Know	N

Number of times met	Abbreviation
Met more than three times	3
Met couple of times	2
Met once	1
Have never met	0

Relationship Status	Abbreviation
Likes my brand and me	RS4
Likes me but not my brand	RS3
Likes my brand but not me	RS2
Not Sure whether he likes my brand or me	RS1

*****

"Business is not just doing deals; business is having great products, doing great engineering, and providing tremendous service to customers. Finally, business is a cobweb of human relationships"

- Ross Perot

Notes

SALES STORY 6.1:

Are you hearing or Listening?

The story of Retail Rashmi

Rashmi was a sales rep at a large retail store, and her job was to sell "Brand S" Smartphones. The "Brand S" was one of the market leaders along with five other brands and was aggressively pushing its retailers and their sales reps to consistently increase not only the unit volumes every month but also the average selling price (ASP) from INR 10000 to INR 12000.The "Brand S" had more than 15 different models of phones starting from a price band of INR 5000 up to INR 25000. Majority of sales were happening in the price band of INR 8000 to INR 12000 thereby delivering as ASP(Average Selling Price) of INR 10000. Their most popular and largest selling model was the "S5 Super" that was available for INR10000 followed by the "S5 Classic" which was available for INR 7000.

To drive the product mix up "Brand S" announced various schemes to retailers and the sales reps on their models priced INR 15000 and higher. They also made it mandatory in the targets of sales reps that 20% of their sales volumes must come from phones priced INR 15000 and more failing which the sales reps stand to lose their incentives. These models were S6 Super, S6 Super Plus, S7 Super and S7 Super Plus.

The biggest challenge of Rashmi was that, though she

was outstanding in taking care of walk-in customers, making high volume sales, she was just not able to scale up the product mix to higher value phones.

One evening, just 15 minutes before the store was to close, a customer walked in. A middle aged person in his mid to late forties, probably returning home from the office.

"Good evening Sir, How can I help you?" Rashmi gave a big smile to the customer

"I am looking for a smartphone." Grunted the middle aged customer looking at the various models displayed on the shelf.

"Great Sir, can I know which price range you are looking for or do you have any specific brand in mind?" asked Rashmi enthusiastically.

"Well, I have heard a lot about "S5 Super". Do you have that phone?

"Yes, Sir. We do have S5 Super"

"What is the best price you can give?" He looked at Rashmi with an expressionless face.

"Sir, it is already priced very aggressively at INR 10000. Let me check with my manager once?" She looked at him tentatively.

"Give me your best price. I will buy right now" the man threw a challenging look across.

Mulling Exercise:

1. *Should Rashmi have answered the customer differently when he asked whether the store has the "S5 Super" phone?*
2. *Why is it essential for salespeople to sell more premium products as part of their portfolio?*

3. *Should a salesperson fulfill customer needs or should the salesperson push different products instead of what the customer is asking for?*

*****

SALES STORY 6.2

First Observe ...then Serve

The meetings of Arvind

Arvind was a sales person with the largest channel partner of a leading lighting company which made smart and internet ready lighting solutions. He was incharge of selling to top corporates in Hyderabad market. Since these were costly solutions and once a corporate bought them they would replicate it to other branch offices, the average deal size for Arvind would be around Rs. 1 Million per deal.

For last 3 months he was working very hard to close the deal for an upcoming multi-storeyed five star International hotel which was coming up near Tank Bund area overlooking the Hussain Sagar lake. This was a very large deal of close to Rs. 1.5M where they were pitching for latest lighting solution along with advanced hardware and software. Arvind's main competitor was a local brand who was importing from China and selling a solution which was cheaper by 30%. The key difference between both the lighting solutions was the software application that Arvind's company was bundling including voice-controlled lighting.

Arvind had given a technical presentation to the Hotel's General Manager and the other stake holders including the Chief of Technical Staff. They all adored the lighting solution and especially the fact that hotel guests can use their voice to switch on, dim, brighten and shut down the lights in their rooms. Similar presentation was also given by the local competitor to the Hotel's decision-making team.

Finally, both the vendors were called for a final negotiation meeting. Arvind requested the Managing Director of the company to accompany him on this crucial meeting. The presence of the senior most person of his company would help showcase the serious intent of theirs to work with the prestigious Hotel.

In the large meeting room sat two directors who were equal owners of the Hotel, along with the Hotel General Manager, Chief of Technical Staff, and Procurement Manager. One of the Directors, was of the opinion that they should just focus on the lighting and fixtures and not waste money on software application that helps to manage and trouble shoot the solution. The second Director was of the opinion that they should invest in the state of art technology and get trained people to manage the lighting of the whole 12 story Hotel from a single control room and that it was worth the money.

As the discussions progressed a small debate between the two power houses broke out in front of Arvind and his MD. The General Manager sensing trouble was trying to say something but could not.....

Mulling Exercise:

1. *What should Arvind and his MD do at this stage?*
2. *How should they take help of the GM who likes their solution?*
3. *How should they justify the premium they are charging over the competition?*
4. *Should Arvind take the side of the Director who is supporting their solution and speak in the meeting?*

DNA Number 6: OBSERVER AND A LISTENER – ABILITY TO UNDERSTAND CUSTOMER NEEDS

Is the job of a sales person that of only fulfilment i.e, give whatever customer asks? Or does the job involve understanding customer needs and providing the best possible solution for the same?

Is it a smart thing to change a customer's mind when he or she has already decided to buy something? Is it not smart to just give whatever the customer is asking and close the sale? Maybe in certain situations, but definitely not in many of the situations. Most of the times, sales persons do not want to RISK losing a sale and take the safe approach of trying to close a sale quickly by giving whatever the customer asks. They are SCARED to suggest something more expensive to the customer in the worry that they will drive away the customer.

Many times, the simple reason is – they only hear the customer speak and react to it. They do not try to UNDERSTAND what the customer says and help customer take the right decision. They do not observe the customer carefully

"A wise old owl lived in an oak
The more he saw the less he spoke
The less he spoke the more he heard.
Why can't we all be like that wise old bird?"

Have you heard this poem before? We associate "Owl" with being "wise" and observant. Owls have large eyes and rarely makes noise around humans. They come and go without anyone knowing or tracking them. They do many of their activities in the night when it is dark. This is when listening and observation becomes more important than seeing.

Similarly, whenever you see someone wise and extremely knowledgeable we always see that they talk less and listen more. Whenever they speak, they are able to exactly communicate what the listener wants to hear and leave everyone around them impressed. Haven't you seen people like these? The creator gave us, human beings, two ears but only one mouth. Isn't this an enough indication that we should be using our ears twice as much as our mouth.

Lets go back to the story of Retail Rashmi.Lets look at two different sales interactions.

....

Scenario 1: Rashmi hears

Customer: Well, I have heard a lot about "Brand S" S5 Super. Do you have that phone?

Rashmi: Yes Sir. We do have S5 Super.

Customer: What is the best price you can give?

Rashmi: Sir, it is already priced very aggressively at INR 10000. Let me check with my manager once?

Customer: Give me your best price. I will buy right now.

What would have happened in the end? Rashmi would have either given the best possible price or would have given something free and billed the phone at INR 10000. Rashmi heard the customer rather than listening to the customer. Could she have done better had she listened to the customer and not just heard and responded?

Let's simulate the conversation again.

……………………..

Scenario 2: Rashmi Listens

Customer: Well, I have heard a lot about "Brand S" S5 Super. Do you have that phone?

Rashmi absorbed the question. *Well, he is entering the shop just before closing and asking specifically about model S5 Super. Does this mean he is in a hurry to buy? Maybe he must go home with a phone today itself. Let's check out*

"Sir, that's a good model Sir. May I know why you are specifically looking at that model Sir?" asked Rashmi

"Well, I have heard good things about that phone and that it has lot of good features. So, I wanted to gift my wife. See, today is our Wedding Anniversary." The man was opening now

Well he has to give a good gift to his wife. Let's push and upsell to him.

"Many congratulations and many many happy returns of the day Sir. Does your wife use the phone a lot Sir and does she like anything in particular in a phone." Rashmi asked enthusiastically.

"Thank you. Well, she uses it for all social media messaging and yes, she loves taking photos and adding all kinds of funny effects to it etc". He replied smiling for the first time.

"Wow, She must be creative Sir. I just need one more help. What is the current phone she is using, and does she complain of any particular issue in the phone frequently" Rashmi was now addressing the PAIN POINT of the customer.

"Well, she uses "Brand M" phone. I don't remember the model. In addition to wanting better quality camera, she is constantly complaining about the battery life." The man replied ACKNOWLEDGING the PAIN POINT.

"Sir, I would seriously suggest you take model S6 Super.

It is just INR 5000 more than S5 Super, but your wife will get – far superior battery life and even more importantly an incredible camera. It will be a genuine upgrade from her existing phone and she will love it like anything. It is not only the latest model but also very solidly built. Whether she is using it in Kitchen or in any environment it will perform beautifully and last for long time" Rashmi confidently put across her VALUE PROPOSITION of the SOLUTION

"Oh! But I was thinking of a INR 10000 budget and this seems to be way more expensive". Her Question got the man thinking.

"Sir, it's your decision finally. If you go with S5 Super, while it is a good phone compared to what your wife is currently using, S6 Super would give a far superior experience to your wife Sir. She will enjoy a premium experience. Also Sir, this is your wedding anniversary. I would suggest that you gift S6 Super and your wife will be extremely thrilled Sir"

"Ok!........ But can you do something on the price?"

"That's not a problem, We have some great EMI Schemes available

Finally the man ended up buying S6 Super. With the Power of listening Retail Rashmi was able to 'upsell' the product, in the process earning more revenue for the company and driving the average selling price higher.

Power of Listening

Did you now understand the power of observation and listening? A slight bit of awareness of the situation, ability to understand what customer is saying, has allowed Rashmi to upsell a INR 10000 customer to INR 15000.

What is the best technique to build your listening skills:

1. Allow customer to complete what he/she wants to say, without interrupting. Sometimes when there are two or more people from the customer side, you can observe a lot about their relationship dynamics when you let them talk, and you only listen.
2. Take a few seconds to understand/appreciate what he/ she said. You can even take notes if the situation permits so that you don't miss out on any point
3. Ask yourself why the customer said whatever he/she said?
4. Summarize the same and ask the customer back for confirmation, to ensure you did not miss out any point.
5. Ask the customer your doubts, queries, or questions to clarify points you did not understand or to start a discussion.Remember, there is never harm in trying. What would be the worst-case scenario after you have tried? The customer would not be convinced and buy the lower priced model itself. However, what happens if you did not ask? You miss out on selling the premium priced model.

Listening changes, the way you sell, and makes you incredibly more successful.

Observation Skills:

"The world is full of obvious things which nobody by any chance ever observes."

There is a classic quote from a Sherlock Holmes book, the world famous fictional detective, who with his sheer observation skills, could find out what the other person is thinking.

Observation is the action or process of closely observing or monitoring something or someone. As a salesperson, what all you must find? Here are a few observation scenarios from real life sales interactions.

1. The behavior of a person in front of you when you are in a meeting.
2. Observe the body language of a person present in the meeting.
3. Two people from the customer side are talking to each other in front of you.
4. You are talking to the customer while he is reading or writing an email.
5. You are talking to the customer while he is calling someone on his phone.
6. You are waiting outside, and the person who came after you goes to meet the customer even before you.
7. Actions of a customer in a store while he or she is browsing the store.
8. The husband and wife are discussing in front of you how much to spend.

You will realize that, instead of talking, you are better at observing and listening. By patiently observing and listening, you will know:

1. What to do next?
2. Who is more powerful among the two people in front of you?
3. How serious are they about buying?
4. Do they like you or not?
5. Do they like your product, proposal, pricing, or not.

Learn to observe. Let's now see what happened in Arvind's meeting.

Arvind and the MD waited patiently waited for both the directors to finish their discussion. Arvind then went on to pitch in line with the second director's argument, i.e. the benefits of having state of the art technology with software control. Then to please the first director, he gave example of a very successful hotel that uses the same solution and is now doing exceptionally well. The Managing Director also promised the first director a decent discount to show their intent on doing that business. Finally, Arvind was able to close the deal and came out as winner. The Managing Director praised him and promoted him!

*****

DNA 6–Ready Reckoner – WRAP Technique for active listening

1. Wait for the person who is talking to you, to complete what they are saying.
2. Repeat whatever you heard, back to the person and get a reconfirmation.
3. Ask the person to clarify any part that you did not understand. Do not assume anything on your own.
4. Play in your mind the whole thing again and ask yourself two things:

a. Why that person is saying this?

b. Why now at this time?

*****

Notes

SALES STORY 7

When Less is More

Ajitabh was a college hire in a big multinational consumer electronics company. He was full of zest, energy and will to win. He would not leave a stone unturned when it came to putting the effort in reaching out to customers, making calls, talking to distributors, having a sales plan. But after putting all the efforts, the sales results that he was getting wasn't as encouraging as it should have been.

Mahesh, who was a senior colleague in the same organization, on the contrary, seem to have a relaxed air about his approach. He would pick and choose a customer, and once he set his eyes on a deal or a customer, he would win most of them! Almost all his sales meetings would end up with customers signing the contract and closing the business for the organization. Mahesh's strike rate was much better than that of Ajitabh! During one of the quarter end team meetings, over a glass of beer, Ajitabh congratulated his senior colleague on the continuous success that he was getting.

"Sir, I am inspired by you." said Ajitabh widening his eyes.

"Thanks, Ajitabh." Mahesh smiled and patted on Ajitabh's shoulder.

"I want to be like you, a champion salesperson" Ajitabh expressed himself earnestly." Sure, My friend, you will be.....is there a problem?" Mahesh asked.

"I fire all my guns, but none of the shots seem to be hitting the right target," Ajitabh told Mahesh about his unyielding efforts in the market.

After patiently listening to Ajitabh, Mahesh gulped his beer and said, " I am going to tell you a secret today."

"What is that?"

Mulling Exercise:

1. *What do you think was Ajitabh's problem?*
2. *What do you think Mahesh was doing to be so successful?*
3. *What should Ajitabh do?*

*****

DNA Number 7: SOLID PRODUCT KNOWLEDGE – KNOWS WHAT TO SELL AND HOW TO SELL

It is essential to have a thorough knowledge of the products, solutions and services that you are selling. Only then you will know how your products solve a customer problem, and you will be able to position the right product or solution.

Before you know about the products you sell, it is fundamental to know about the following:

- Your company and Your brand.
- Your industry.
- The market you are selling to.
- The primary technology or the engineering or the science or the story behind what you are selling.
- Knowing about industry standards, certifications, regulatory compliances, rules etc.
- Characteristics of your customer.
- Different popular customer profiles who would need your product.
- Why do customers need your product? What benefits or value it brings to their day to day lives or business operations?
- Reference list of your company's top existing customers and how your products are helping these customers run their businesses or solve their day to day problems.

In short, you should know about your business end to end.

1. **About your company and brand**:

Everything starts with knowing about your company and the brand. Only a salesperson who loves his company and brand can talk about its products passionately to customers and communicate the benefits effectively.

a. Who was the founder?

b. When did it start?

c. Any fascinating facts and stories about your company and brand that makes you feel very proud to work for that company and brand.

d. How many patents & innovations does your company have?

e. What were the first inventions or creations of your company?

f. What were your company's first products?

g. Who are your company's marquee customers? How many customers does your company serve?

h. What's your company's pedigree?

i. What all awards have your company won?

j. Who is the current CEO, CFO, CMO, etc.?

k. In how many cities, towns, countries your company is present in?

l. How many employees and channel partners you have?

m. How many service centres across the country?

2. **About your industry**:

About the industry, that your company and your product belongs to? Ex. If you joined in selling automobiles, you must have a reasonable idea about the automobile industry. If you are selling telecom solutions, you should know about the telecom industry.

a. How big is this industry?

b. Who are the key players?

c. What is the ranking and positioning of your company compared to its competitors in the industry?

d. What all products, solutions and services constitute your industry?

e. What are the characteristics of your industry? Is it a domestic manufacturing industry or an import based industry?

f. Is there any industry body which represents and guides the industry, e.g. SIAM works closely with Automobile Industries, NASSCOM works with software companies etc.

3. **The market you are selling to**:

You need to know where your customers are, what segment they belong to, what is the nature of their business, what is their buying behavior, how do they buy and how you are going to target them.

Your market classification could be based on:

a. Geography.i.e.

  i. A small territory, (Ex. South Delhi),

  ii. Larger Area (Delhi),

  iii. More prominent Region (Delhi NCR),

  iv. Complete Zone (North India),

  v. Total Country (India).

b. Industry vertical i.e

  i. Manufacturing companies in that geography.

  ii. Educational Institutions in that geography.

  iii. Banking, Financial Services and Insurance companies in that geography.

iv. IT/ITES and Telecom companies in that geography.

v. State Government, Central Government organizations.

vi. Public Sector Companies. Defense Industry companies.

c. Customer Size

i. Small business customers with 1 to 100 employees.

ii. Medium business customers with 101 to 500 employees.

iii. Large business customers with 501 to 1000 employees.

iv. Very Large Enterprise business customers with more than 1000 employees.

4. **Buying characteristics of your customers**:

Depending on the type of customers you target, you will find that they exhibit common characteristics.

a. E.g. Core Govt customers like Ministries buy in a particular way, whereas Public Sector organizations buy differently.

b. Similarly, Defense services procure differently.

c. Software companies exhibit a similar type of buying characteristics, whereas Call Centers exhibit an entirely different set of buying characteristics.

You should be able to fine tune your product pitch accordingly.

5. **The type of person you are interacting with–different popular customer profiles who you would be interacting with while selling your product**:

Within the above customer organizations you will find different customer profiles like

i. People from Purchase department – Purchase Manager, Procurement Executive etc.
ii. People from the IT department – CIO, IT Manager, MIS Manager, Data Admin etc.
iii. Office Administration Manager
iv. People from finance department – CFO, Finance Manager, Finance Executive etc.
v. People from Engineering team–Engineering Head, Engineers etc.
vi. Senior most Management team – CEO, MD, Directors etc.
vii. People from marketing team – CMO, Marketing Head, marketing manager etc.
viii. People from the sales team – CSO, Sales Head, Zonal Manager, Circle Manager, Regional Manager, Area Manager etc.
ix. People from other teams – Designers, Software Engineers, Project Managers
x. Different type of users

Each of the above people behave in a particular way. When you pitch your product to each person, you need to talk the language he or she understands and address the issues faced by them.

For ex. The CFO is interested in lower running cost. The Purchase Manager is interested in lower acquisition cost. The IT Manager is interested in ensuring maximum uptime and minimal complaints from his users so that his life can become better.

The Sales Head wants to ensure the equipment used by his sales team is easy to use and helps them become more productive. Similarly, each user wants the best possible product for using in his day to day work that will make their life more comfortable and perform their job better.

a. Similarly, in retail, different popular profiles of customers walk-in.

    i. High Net worth Individuals.
    ii. Families with children.
    iii. Students.
    iv. Business Men and Professionals.
    v. Young couples etc.

Each of them behaves in a particular way, and it is essential for the salesperson to fine tune his pitch accordingly.

6. **The fundamental technology or the engineering or the science or the story behind what you are selling**:

To be effective in sales, it is not enough to just know about your product. You should see the reason behind how your product came into being and how it works in real life to benefit customers. You should know how the technology or engineering or science behind the product you are selling has evolved. What benefits has this brought to customers?

a. A financial services salesperson should know about how interest rates are calculated, what is PLR, repo rate etc. depending on the type of customer he or she is interacting with.

b. A car salesman should have a basic idea about how a petrol engine works or a diesel engine works. He should be able to understand the technology behind AMT technology so that it would help him articulate the cause of an auto-car over a manual car more convincingly to the customer.

c. A Smartphone salesperson should have proper idea about different technologies that drive a smartphone like, OS–

iOS/Android, two or three additional benefits customer will get with the new Android OS compared to the earlier version. What does ppi mean in display technology and how does this help a customer? What is Megapixel, and what role does it play in a camera?Similarly, a computer salesperson should know the basics of processor technology, memory technology, storage technology etc.

7. **Knowing about industry standards, certifications, regulatory compliances, rules etc.**:

Knowing about industry standard norms to ensure the customer is buying as per recommended standards.

a. Ex. a real estate salesperson should know about RERA approvals, Municipal Corporation Approvals, Other Legal Clearances etc.

b. Ex. Knowing about emission standards is essential when you selling equipment needing environmental certifications.

c. When a customer is buying a product with chemical properties, it important about guiding the customer and ensuring he gets a product that has RoHS (Reduction of Hazardous Substances) certification. When selling financial services, making sure that customer is getting products that adhere to regulatory norms and no wrong selling is happening.

8. **Giving the reference of existing customers**

Always try and share the reference list of your company's top existing customers, who are using the same products and how your products are helping these customers run their businesses or solve their day to day problems – Majority of customers are conservative. They buy what majority buy. They buy tried and tested. When you give references to a customer about other customers who are using the same product or service that this customer is considering, they feel comfortable and buy the same.

9. **The most important point of all–Why do customers need your product, i.e. what benefits it brings to their day to day lives**?

   This is the most essential part of product knowledge. If you are a person with in-depth knowledge of the product you are selling, the industry you belong to and the customer you are selling to, you can do three things:

a. You will be able to understand how your product can help solve different types of problems faced by different types of customers, which means you can pitch the right product to the right customer.
b. Secondly, if you can understand how your product can help enhance the quality of life or user experience or performance or productivity of the customer, you can even pitch a better product to customer and increase your revenue.
c. Thirdly if you can understand how your product can help the customer grow their business by being more competitive in the market and beat their competition, then your customer will buy whatever you sell.

FAB Technique for pitching a product:

Best way to sell a product is to use the FAB technique, i.e. Features, advantages and benefits technique. Every product has various features, big and small, tangible and intangible. It is important to translate these product features into how advantageous these features are to the customer. This can be done by explaining or demonstrating to the customer how easy it is to use and maintain the product and thereby translate to "real life benefits" that makes customer life easy.

Feature– Feature is a physical characteristic or a function that is present or visible in your product or service.

This is quantifiable and checked.

Advantage– Advantage is a functional characteristic that can show the customer, how a particular feature translates into performance when customer is using it. It shows a customer, how easy it is to use that feature and the product. Typically the best way of showing this is by demonstrating the product or even better, letting the customer try it out. Ex. Customer taking a test drive before buying a vehicle.

Benefit– Benefit is the answer to customer's question, "What is in it for me?". How is this going to make my life easy or better? The sales person can answer this to the customer more easily once customer tries the product features himself/herself and gets comfortable with it.

Now, going back to the sales story, here is what Mahesh told Ajitabh:

"How many quotes have you given in the last one-week Ajitabh? Asked Mahesh

"About ten to twelve quotes" Ajitabh replied confidently

"Hmmm...What is the status of these deals? How many are closing this month?" Mahesh asked after a pause looking straight at Ajitabh's eyes

"Unfortunately, other than one deal, I cannot forecast the status of all other deals?" Ajitabh replied sheepishly

"Why did you give so many quotes Ajitabh? What was the need? Did you understand the exact need of the customer before sending these quotes or you just responded to customer requests? How sure are you that, whatever products you have quoted meets customer needs perfectly?" Mahesh threw a barrage of questions at Ajitabh

"Well....I thought by sending quotes I am proactively seeding information to the customer which will help me.." Ajitabh replied in a low tone

"No Ajitabh. You are only wasting your valuable time. Remember the golden rule, ***"for every unqualified prospect you are spending time on, you are missing out on a qualified prospect"*** said Mahesh

"So, what should I do?

"Study the requirement thoroughly. Meet different stakeholders in your prospect organization. Only when you qualify the customer's *intent* to purchase you must move to the next step of positioning the right product and giving a proposal. If you are unable to answers the below questions, there is no point in giving a quote" concluded Mahesh.

There was a momentary silence as if the wisdom was sinking in Ajitabh's mind. Mahesh smiled and then continued," Remember this Ajitabh, before sending a quote you should always check the following.

- Is it an existing customer and if not, are they at least customer's of a similar brand like ours?
- If they are a new company/start-up, how are they funded?
- Is there a genuine need from customer side?
- Does customer have the financial capability to buy?
- Even if he has the need and the capability, can we as a brand participate in the opportunity, considering our price premiums and payment terms?

Once you have qualified the opportunity correctly and positioned the right product, you can then give a quote. You will realize that your conversion rate increases dramatically."

"Thank you so much Mahesh Sir…this is helpful" a radiant smile spilled over Ajitabh's face.

Knowing your product well and most importantly knowing how and when to sell it is very important. No wonder, Mahesh is a Champion Sales Person.

******

DNA 7–Ready Reckoner – FAB Technique

Features	Advantages	Benefits
Physical Characteristic	**Functional Characteristic**	**What's in it for the customer**
Examples		
64GB Storage	Customer can store up to 10000 photos, 8000 documents, 3000 songs and 1000 videos at same time	Never run out of space; Save a lot of time because all data in one place; Total peace of mind
Service Support App	Customer can log complaints any time of the day and track the status	Save time logging in complaints; Be aware of the status any time
Leather Seats	Silky, smooth feel when you sit; looks very premium and expensive; Long life	Comfortable experience of sitting; Higher resale value; Show off with pride to friends and family; Low running cost
3 years warranty	Assured parts, labour and onsite service for three years from purchase date	No additional money to be spent for next three years. Peace of mind for next three years;

******

DNA 7–Self-Exercise by Mr./Ms :____________

Take any of the products you sell, please put down the features of the product and write the advantages and benefits.

Features	Advantages	Benefits
Physical Characteristic	**Functional Characteristic**	**What's in it for the customer**

Notes

SALES STORY 8

Talk Right or Talk Relevant?

You can't sell anything if you can't tell anything

~ Beth Comstock

When Venugopal, who was almost 10 years old in a leading FMCG company was invited to present during one of the sessions in the induction training of a bunch of newly recruited MBA graduates, he could hardly believe his senses. *I am a simple commerce graduate who moved into field sales 10 years ago. I have not studied management subjects like "Brand Positioning" or "Consumer Behavior" what can I teach these bright minds.* With these doubts in his mind, Venugopal walked upto his Manager, Mr Swamy.

"Sir, why me? he asked. Venugopal has spent most of his sales career working under Mr Swamy.

Mr. Swamy looked at his face, and with a smile replied, "Venu, I understand your apprehensions, but tell me something. In the last few years who has got the best sales champion award for the south region?"

"Sir, I have got this award three years in a row now" Venu replied enthusiastically."And do you know the reason why?" asked Mr Swamy

"Sir because of my hard work" replied Venugopal.

"It is indeed your hard work Venu, but have you noticed what is your biggest strength?"

Venugopal was deep in thought, Mr Swamy broke the silence and said, "It's your ability to communicate effectively with almost everyone. Be it your customers or the dealers or their sales agents."Venugopal smiled. After a brief pause he said, "Sir, It never occurred to me as my strength. I was a naturally outgoing personality since childhood. Probably that's the reason why I am in sales at the first place. How can I teach these young kids how to communicate?" Mr Swamy looked at him and calmly said, "Communication is a skill that you can learn, it's like riding a bicycle or swimming. If one is willing to work on it, he or she can improve this skill."

Mulling Exercise:

1. *How did Venugopal become so good in communications?*
2. *Why is it essential for freshers to learn from senior people?*
3. *Are people good in communications from a young age, or can they become good communicators by practice?*

DNA Number 8: ORATOR – ABILITY TO COMMUNICATE EFFECTIVELY IN DIFFERENT FORUMS

A good Orator makes us see with our ears ~ Arabic Proverb

What is common between

MK Gandhi

Abraham Lincoln

Martin Luther King

Barack Obama

Atal Bihari Vajpayee

Narendra Modi

All of them are great Orators!

Are we born Orators? Yes and No both.

Yes, because every human being can talk and express themselves, but the ability to express themselves effectively in a way that would make another human getting moved by communication is an art. This art can be learned, practiced and improved upon.

Barrister MK Gandhi lost his first case. But the man later became 'the father of nation' Mahatma Gandhi and propelled India's freedom movement with the help of his oratory skills backed by his actions.

Lincoln's voice was not exactly music to ears, he spoke in a shrill, squeaking, voice. His general look, his form, his pose, his sensitiveness, and his momentary shyness, everything seemed to be against him, but he soon recovered. He spent many years polishing his speaking abilities, from his youth to his presidency. His life in politics gave him hundreds of opportunities, as did his 25-year law career.

Martin Luther King's famous speech "I Have a Dream" was delivered without any notes, and he improvised much of it on the spot. He worked on much of the content of that speech in other addresses he gave months and years before the "March on Washington for Jobs and Freedom" in 1963.

Atal Bihari Vajpayee's speech in Hindi in UN General Assembly in 1977 as a new comer to the united nations was one of the finest ever and reflected a young nation's brewing confidence and a significant image change as the world looked at Indians

What do we mean by communications?

It means our ability to put forward information either verbally, or in writing or through facial expressions or body language or in combination of any of those four ways to our audience. Our audience could be just one person in front, more than one person in front, or one or more recipients of your letter, email or text message.

What do we want to achieve by communicating?

We want to convey our point of view or our thoughts or information so that we can achieve one or more of the below results:

- Convince your audience on your points of view.
- Pass on information that will have value to your audience.
- Help enable your audience and recipients of your information to effectively act on it and revert to you back.
- Get confirmation on something that will help you achieve your goals.
- Simply build a strong relationship between you and your audience.

- Communicate how smart or capable or helpful you are.
- Get help to manage a crisis.
- Help someone in crisis.

Exercise:

Make a list of various people you communicate with, on daily basis on what type of communication you use to interact with them:

Person or Persons Communicated with	Type of Communication (Verbal, Non-Verbal or Written)	Formal or Informal Communication	Objective of the communication	Impact on your personal or work life (High, Medium, Low)
Father	Verbal	Informal	Whether he took medicines or not	Medium
Uber Driver	Verbal	Formal	To align with him on your pick up	Low
Your Colleague	Verbal	Informal	Wished her Good Morning	Low
Your CEO	Verbal	Formal	Wished her Good Morning	High
Your Customer	Written	Formal	Sent the Commercial Proposal	High
Your Customer	Written	Formal	Texted reconfirming meeting time	High

Your Customers	Written	Formal	Forwarded new product EDM	High
Your dealers	Verbal	Formal	Did a 30 minute presentation on the new scheme	High
Your dealers	Verbal	Informal	Interactions during cocktails	High

Use the template at Chapter end and make a list as above:

Communications can be broken broadly into the following two types

1. Formal and Informal communications.
2. Written, Verbal and Non-Verbal Communications.

Formal Communications:

When communicating with someone related to your professional or personal life but with the objective of achieving important results. That requires an orderly interaction following right protocols and societal norms.

Few Examples:

- Interacting with a customer for the business.
- Interacting with a medical expert on understanding the diagnosis of a medical problem.
- Inviting an elderly relative or dignitary for a family function or a business event.

Informal Communications:

When communicating with someone, you know so well, and they don't expect you to follow any formal protocols or societal norms.

Few Examples:

- Chatting with friends and family
- Talking to a customer or dealer in a casual environment (*It's the best thing that can happen in a customer relationship)*

Written Communications:

Written Communication: could be hand written on a paper, email or word or PowerPoint document or a text message, or an image created on a smartphone etc.

Verbal Communications:

Live conversations with one or more people either face to face or on Skype.

Lectures, Seminars and Presentations delivered to a small or large group of audience either face to face or through Webinars, recorded messages and videos etc.

Non-Verbal Communications:

Communicating your happiness or anguish, demonstrating something in front of people using your body expressions and work. Typically, non-verbal communication is used in combination with verbal communications to increase the impact of the interactions.

Now coming to sales, effective communications are the back bone for a salesperson. **As Seth Godin says, "People do not buy goods and services. They buy relations, stories and magic."** So salesperson is not just selling a product. He is selling his relationship value to the customer, the benefits that will make customer's life better and improve customer's life and business significantly.

Let us get more specific and look at three crucial communication areas for a salesperson that he or she has to master to be successful in sales:

1. Communicating through telephone.
2. Face to Face communications during meetings with customers and with internal stakeholders.
3. Written Communications to customers and with internal stakeholders.

Communicating through telephone

Communicating through the telephone is the lifeline of a salesperson. The phone is your go to gadget that can get you through to your customer be it to fix that urgent appointment, discuss areas and subject of conversations, work on action points etc.

Selling through telephone saves the most valuable resource in the world, "TIME". In today's world physically commuting from one place to another might take time and can affect your productivity. Effective communication on the telephone can solve multiple problems. People may say if it is about saving time and money, why not email or text message? Why a verbal conversation on a telephone or a video conferencing on a PC? The reason is – oral communications are not only about the voice and the choice of words, you also *talk* through your facial expressions, voice modality that is crucial in clarifying important doubts, that an email or a text message cannot.

When we meet face to face, because of the time spent, we end up covering most of the discussion topics and recover from mistakes to communicate the key points in the right manner. However, on the phone, since we get very little time, we need to ensure two critical things – quality of conversation, completeness of discussion.

1. How to ensure completeness of the conversation. You guarantee completeness by being **PROMPT**. What is **PROMPT**?

I. Prepare
II. Rehearse
III. On-time
IV. Maximize
V. Persuade
VI. Thank

2. How to ensure conversation quality and impact on the listener. This can only happen when you make **PEPSI** your habit. What is **PEPSI**?
   I. Passion for your brand
   II. Eager to discuss
   III. Patience to pause and listen
   IV. Suggest with conviction
   V. In with a smile

Combination of PEPSI and PROMPT will ensure highly effective telephone selling.

Communicating Face to Face

Napoleon Bonaparte said, "We rule the world by our words".

This becomes extremely important for face to face meetings.

For effective communications during face to face meetings, the salesperson needs to be well prepared? Please find below a checklist for "preparing for a face to face meeting"

S.No	Preparation Checklist for effective face to face meetings
1	Who are you meeting?
2	When are you meeting?

3	Where are you meeting?
4	What are you going to talk about?
5	What materials/documentation/presentations would you need?
6	Why are you meeting?
7	What is your expectation from the meeting?

Once you are prepared and enter a face to the meeting or an event, you need to remember the following:

1. Personal grooming and hygiene.
2. Business card etiquettes.
3. Observing the customer.
4. Organizing your speech or the topic you want to talk about.
5. DO's and DON'Ts.

Personal grooming and hygiene

- Style hair carefully.
- Dress like a professional.
- Shake hands firmly and look people in the eye.
- Business card etiquettes

Business card etiquette when you are giving:

- Readily available, preferably in a dedicated holder.
- Neat & clean card.
- Hand it over with both hands or right hand.
- Text facing the customer.
- Your name/company name should be visible.
- Ensure any changed information like phone no/ designation etc.Is already done and not in front of the customer.

Business card etiquette when you are receiving:

- Receive it like you are receiving a gold biscuit.
- Keep it face-up in front of you till the meeting is over.

Observing the customer

- Is customer interested in what you are saying?
- Makes you wait.
- Asking you to carry on while he or she is talking with someone else.
- Doing something else in parallel.
- Is customer getting impatient/annoyed with what you are saying?
- Interrupting you as you are saying something.
- Is customer focused on what you are saying?
- Is the customer sitting relaxed and leaning back.
- Gets you a tea or coffee.

Organizing your speech or the topic you want to talk about

- Focus on the main points.
- If you are passionate about something, be prepared with right script and examples. Otherwise you could get garbled.
- Make it clear on what you wish to convey from the outset.
- Stay on the topic. Don't divert attention.
- Thank your listeners.

DO's and DON'Ts

- Set the listener at ease.
- Be articulate.
- Avoid mumbling.

- Be attentive while listening.
- Be vocally interesting – change the tone/pitch.

Make Sure you practice and follow the above shared points regularly. Find a friend or a colleague with whom you can practice some of these tips and improve considerably as an orator and an effective communicator.

Written Communications to customers

1. ***Email Communications:***

1.1 Subject Line–Always have a subject line that reflects the contents of an email the message. Only then people marked in the email will straightaway understand and act on it.

- For example, if the e-mail is about your proposal for a surveillance solution for a hospitality client, the subject should be – "Proposal for surveillance solution for your upcoming new hotel"
- If the e-mail is about your upcoming meeting with a client to discuss requirement in detail, the subject should be–"Meeting to discuss requirement."
- If the e-mail is requesting for leave, the subject should be – "Leave Request"

1.2 Short and Simple Sentences–Use short and easy sentences. Each sentence should not be more than one or two lines. Remember, you are not writing essays and thesis. You are communicating with customers and internal teams to get answers, communicate your points and get answers. People will get bored if they see long messages with long and complex sentences. If you want to convey more things, use bullet point and sequence out each point one by one in short and simple sentences.

Remember KISS – Keep It Short and Simple

1.3 Use Positive words

USE words like: *helpful, good question, agreed, together, useful, I'd be delighted, mutual, opportunity etc.*

DON'T USE words like *busy, crisis, failure, forget it, I can't, it's impossible, waste, hard, deal etc.*

Positive words give hope and confidence. Also, it doesn't hurt ego of the recipient incase that person is senior and expects respect. Negative words come across like ultimatums and even hurts egos.

1.4 Be very careful of capital letters, punctuation, spelling and basic grammar

While these can be tolerated in informal emails, they are essential in business emails as they are an important part of the image you create.

1.5 Ensure correct email addresses of the recipients:

Please ensure you type in the right email addresses of the recipients. Due to 'autocomplete function', many times you end up sending emails to wrong people. One option is to disable the "autocomplete' feature. This will ensure you consciously type in the email IDs of your customers correctly.

1.6 Handle attachments with care:

Firstly ensure you don't send the email and forget to add the attachment. This is a common mistake that many people make. They will reply all on the already sent email with a body copy which says… "Sorry missed, the attachment". What happens is, the recipients will open the attachment but not go thru the complete cover note/email body copy you sent earlier. The impact of your email reduces drastically.

Secondly, ensure, you send the right attachment. Always click open the attachment, satisfy to yourself that it is the right attachment and then only press the "send" button.

Many times people send the right attachment to the wrong person and wrong attachment to the right person.

1.7 Edit the email before sending:

Give yourself time to edit what you've written before you push that Send button.

In today's busy world, it's common for people to send out many emails without checking them. You should make a conscious effort to edit. Due to the "autocorrect" feature, many times words get auto corrected by the software, and they are not what you want. Ideally, we recommend that you disable "autocorrect" feature to ensure you put in the right words that make an impact. Also run a grammar check and spell check to provide your email professional eligibility. This reflects on your brand and yourself positively.

2. ***Proposals:***

Significant proposals reflect great brands and great salespersons. An excellent proposal will outline customer requirement clearly, the solution that fits the requirement, the commercials including terms and conditions and all of this supported by – justifications to the solution suggested, key benefits to the customer, unique value proposition which says why you are better than the competition and reference customers or proof concept details.

Depending on customers, the product or solution or services sold, the proposals can range from pre-printed pamphlets (incase of retail products), customized documents, detailed powerpoint presentations, proof of concept results etc.

Tips for great proposals:

2.1 Know your customer and customer requirement thoroughly

2.2 Connect the proposal to the previous discussions and meetings you have had with the customer. Summarize them on a cover page or covering email when you are sending the proposal.

2.3 Communicate how your product or solution can deliver the benefits that customer is looking at.

2.4 Be very clear on your deliverables. It is always better to under commit and over deliver than over commit and under deliver.

2.5 Share details of reference customers and success stories with your customer so that they will be more confident about you and your proposal.

2.6 Make sure you are addressing the proposal to the correct person and sharing it with all key decision makers and influencers.

2.7 Give a fair price. Do not discount yourself upfront nor rate yourself artificially high. Quote what you believe you are worth and depending on the competition and the customer buying behavior.

2.8 Make your proposal visually appealing with clear fonts, tables, colors and pictures where required. Don't make a short and drab proposal when the customer is investing so much time, effort and money.

2.9 Always cross check multiple times before you send it out.

2.10 Create attractive design templates for your proposals and standardize them. This will ensure that you don't need to spend a lot of time every time you have to make a proposal. You should be focussing on the content and not on making it beautiful every single time.

3. Smartphone Communications

Nowadays we tend to communicate a lot on Smartphones, be it using SMS, WhatsApp, Email etc. We have started using Smartphones extensively for even business and official purposes.

There are many advantages of Smartphone communications. Some of them are:

- Ability to send message directly to decision makers and approvers.
- Ability to send messages anytime of the day.
- Ability to send messages on the move from anywhere.

However, we also run the risk of:

- Typographical and autocorrect errors.
- Improper salutations and disrespectful language.
- Using smileys and short forms.
- Incomplete information.
- Sending to wrong numbers/persons.
- Sending messages at inappropriate times.
- Losing critical information since phone is easily misplaced or stolen or accidental deletion of data.

It is important to ensure the following when sending information through Smartphone:

1. Address the customer by proper title (Mr. / Ms / Hon'ble / Sir / Ma'am etc) even if it is SMS or WhatsApp
2. Start with proper Salutation – Respected Sir, Hello Ma'am, Dear Mr. etc.
3. Give space between important points.
4. Sign off with your full name, designation, email etc.
5. Spell check and grammar check.

It is important to avoid:

1. Smileys and Abbreviations.
2. Sending messages at odd times (unless critical).
3. Spamming without permission.

*****

Going back to Venugopal's experience, he gave a great talk on communication skills to the new joiners. He gave many great examples of real life situations, wherein he used his communication convince internal and external customers to decide in favour of him. Even though he was not from a top tier university or institute, because of the communication skills, he became successful in his career.

Communication skills are not something people are born with. One can become an excellent communicator with practice and passion.

*****

DNA 8–Ready Reckoner – Communication Techniques Telephone Communication Skills

PROMPT Technique to ensure you complete your conversation with your customer without missing any point.

Prepare

Rehearse

On-time

Maximize

Persuade

Thank

PEPSI Technique to ensure conversation quality and impact on the listener.

Passion for your brand.

Eager to discuss.

Patience to pause and listen.

Suggest with conviction.

In with a smile.

DNA 8–Self-Exercise by Mr./Ms:______________

For different types of communication, identify your strengths and areas of improvements. (up to 5 per type of communication)

What are things I am currently doing right	**What are the areas I need to improve**
Telephonic Communications	
Face To Face Meetings	
Written Communications	

Smartphone Communications	

Notes

SALES STORY 9

Win-Win or Win-Lose or Lose-Win or Lose-Lose?

Chiranjib Banerjee was an experienced sales manager at a leading engineering equipment manufacturing company supplying to various manufacturing industries, who buys their machinery and use it in their manufacturing and production processes. He was based out of Kolkata handing customers in Eastern India geographical region.

The challenge that Chiranjib faced was always on price. Finding the right price to sell was always difficult for him. The price at which company wanted to sell the products was not what the customers wanted to buy the products at, and similarly the price at which customers wanted to buy was not the price at which company wanted to sell its products to the market.

As a result, the discounting could go as high as up to 50% on their quoted price before the customers would finalize the purchase. Many factors that lead to negotiations

- Aggressive discounting pricing policy followed by competition.
- A constant customer drive to reduce their input costs.
- Long payment terms wherein customers would want to get up to 180 days credit.

Chiranjib always found it difficult to negotiate a price to sell the product that would include all what customer wanted and would still be profitable for the firm. Most of the business awarded to him was because of his long term relationship with the clients and at times out of sheer desperation to meet the revenue needs of the firm he would go ahead and match the customer target price and credit terms.

While his management was not happy with him, they were also unable to do anything because they needed a loyal employee in East India. However it was always after so much haggling and to and fros that Chiranjib's deals got approved. Because of this, his management was also not excited to invest in East India and grow that business. The company was stuck at status quo as far as East business was concerned.

Chiranjib was a great communicator, had excellent product knowledge, had good operational experience and yet was unable to close deals that are win-win to both his organization and the customer. Most of his deals were win-lose: a win for the customer but a bad deal for his organization.

Mulling Exercise:

1. *What was Chiranjib's issue?*
2. *How should he get out of this situation and move to a win-win situation?*
3. *Should the company shut down its east operations or get a new person?*

*****

DNA Number 9: MASTER NEGOTIATOR – ENSURES WIN-WIN FOR BOTH CUSTOMER AND THE ORGANIZATION

	BRAND WINS	BRAND LOSES
CUSTOMER WINS	**WIN-WIN**	**WIN-LOSE**
CUSTOMER LOSES	**LOSE-WIN**	**LOSE-LOSE**

What do you mean by Win-Win negotiations?

It means the customer gets what he/she wants and is very happy and brand receives the kind of sale it wants, be it price or profits or timely payment or market share or share of wallet or a Prestigious customer for reference use. Ideally Win-Win means the brand is selling at a profitable price which allows them to run a good business.

What are the benefits of Win-Win agreements?

Both parties are happy. The customer gets the right product, excellent service and great support.

Brand or Companies can sustain a healthy business and take good care of customers and employees. Salespeople can make incentives and get salary increases timely.

What happens with Win-Lose or Lose-Lose agreements?

Let us look at it from seller's perspective: The party (seller) which loses starts losing interest in taking care of the other party (buyer) over a period of time. Their margins and profits come down, and this slowly erodes their quality of after sales service and new product quality. Good employees start leaving the company. Also reputation of the brand starts taking a beating in the market which would drive away customers. History is full of examples of many companies which have sold at low or no margins and have ended up shutting down.

Let us look at it from buyer perspective:

In their push for discounts, many customers who ended up buying harmful products at wrong prices have ended up suffering and have changed suppliers. Also many customers who delay supplier payment inordinately and even default in few cases slowly start losing reputation in the market as the right customer. Soon good brands stop selling to these customers in fear of losing money. These customers start to buy from inferior brands, poor quality products and over a period of time this start affecting their business. Many companies which have indulged in such practices have ended up shutting down.

How to achieve and negotiate a win-win understanding?

The moment we talk negotiations, everyone assumes it is about the price. Yes, while price negotiation is very important, *there are other things a sales rep must negotiate* before even getting into price negotiations. If the sales rep does these series of negotiations smartly the pressure on price negotiations decrease significantly. What are these series of negotiations:

1. *Negotiating* to meet the *right* person.
2. *Negotiating* to meet the *right* person at the customer place at the right time.
3. *Negotiating* to meet the *right* person at the right time at the right place.
4. *Negotiating* and *agreeing* on the *right* product and solution.
5. *Negotiating* a *confirmation* from the customer that the

product you have quoted is good.

6. *Negotiating* a *confirmation* from the customer that there is no issue with your brand.
7. *Negotiating* a *confirmation* from the customer that there is no issue with your service support.

All these are called ***Preventive Negotiations***. If we do these preventive negotiations smartly, then you can drive a win-win relationship with the customer. There will be a less need for curative negotiations which will mainly revolve around price and commercial terms and conditions.

There are four key aspects of negotiations:

1. **Preventive negotiation**:

Negotiating and pushing forward various factors that create a favourable environment for the salesperson. E.g.. If you meet the right person at the customer place at right time.

- You ensure that you can probe better and uncover the right needs, which means you can quote the right product or solution upfront rather than by trial and error and revising your proposal multiple times.
- You will be able to understand the milestones in customer procurement process clearly from the decision maker himself or herself, which means you know what you need to do at each stage.
- You will have precise inputs about various stakeholders involved and plan your relationship strategy within customer organization.

2. **Every Small Thing Matters (ESTM) Negotiation**:

One of the key things to remember when negotiating with any customer is the fact that every small thing matters. Never *assume* anything from your side is trivial. What is trivial to you may not be trivial to customer. It could be of incredible value to customer. Ex. Product, Special features, Upgrade, Attach accessories, Delivery, Warranty, Installation, Buy-back, Payment Terms, additional services etc.

Let's take a couple of detailed examples.

- You can easily supply your product in ten different colors, and hence it doesn't matter if customer chooses any of the ten colors. But imagine from a customer side, whose corporate logo, theme, campus is all in blue color, and they buy everything blue and only blue. If you are the only one who can supply blue color product within stipulated deadline, customer will end up buying only from you.
- You have a lot of inventory and can deliver ex-stock. So, for you, delivery is not an issue. Your focus and pressure are all on getting business. Imagine a customer having 20 new employees joining in 3 days and if he does not have your product within three days, the employees will be idle leading to colossal productivity and motivation issues. This customer will pay premium for getting immediate deliveries whereas for you, sitting on huge inventory, quick delivery is not of any concern. If you are smart, you will get customer to give you a better price or better payment terms.
- Many times, especially in retail stores, salespeople do not realize the value of ESTM. There is a customer who will pay full price for getting product delivered on a particular day because it is the birthday of their special ones or wedding anniversary etc. Without probing, what reason the customer is buying for, the retail salesperson gives away discounts unnecessarily.
- Giving 30 days credit may be a reasonable thing to you because your company is comfortable with it. If you had opened your mouth and told the customer, "Sir, for 30

days credit we charge 1.5% extra, at least one out of ten customers would have told you, "No problem. 30 days credit is important to me. I will pay you 1.5% extra" ...

The Problem is, most of the salespeople don't *try* the ESTM technique consistently. You must try it with 100% of your customers. Even if 20% give you better deal, you are adding value to your organization. Your margins increase. Your revenues increase. Your profits increase. Always remember ESTM. What is small to you, maybe, is big to a customer.

3. **Give Value Not Discount (GVND)**

Another very important factor to remember is that you can always trade value for the price. The cost could be better delivery, better payment terms, better product etc. It could be anything that is seen by customer as valuable, but for you it is cost wise cheaper than offering a discount.

Instead of matching customer target price, meet customer halfway and for the balance half, give value. Some examples below:

- *"Sorry Sir. I cannot give any discount since we have limited supply of this model and there is lot of demand. For you, as a special case, I will do installation free of cost. I will not charge you for it."*
- *"Sorry Sir. I cannot give any discount since we have limited supply of this model and there is lot of demand. For you, as a special case, I will do installation free of cost. I will not charge you for it."*
- *"Ma'am, I have already given the best possible price. What I can do for you is, I will make myself available for an extra half a day to help your team complete their assignment and guide them. I will not charge you for this."*

- *"Sir, We cannot give further price discount. However, as a special case, we can extend your warranty by 12 months from 1 year to 2 years. That would give you total peace of mind*".
- *"Ma'am, We cannot upgrade you to business class at the same price. However, we can put you up in the emergency exit row with extended leg room. Would that interest you?"*

4. **Long term Lock-up (LTL)negotiation**:

Here you strive for long term agreements, rate contract and schemes with the customer rather than a transactional piece-meal approach. Instead of trying to close a sale now and then, you sign a Quarterly, Half-yearly or annual agreements. For e.g

- *Sir, since this is a special price, can we sign a rate contract for six months or up to 1000 units whichever is earlier so that you are assured of product availability and I can forecast with 100% commitment to my factory and keep material available for you.*
- *Sir, I can agree to this price if you confirm that you will give us a minimum ten million rupees business in the next 12 months.*
- *"Sir, I can agree to this price, provided there is no price revision for the next 6 months*"
- *"Sir, if you give us more than ten million business in the next six months, our company will upgrade you to platinum service which means you will get free warranty for additional one year on all your purchases."*
- *"Ma'am if you cross Rupees 50 million advertisement business in 12 months, we will give you three full page advertisements free in January next year"*

Remember the above four type of negotiation

techniques to ensure you always drive a win-win agreement with your customers and keep your organization also happy.

Let's go back to Chiranjib's story.

Finally, his management realized the only way to get Chiranjib to negotiate better was to create schemes and offers; So they gave him plans and offers like:

- *Deals with 100% advance will get ex-stock delivery.*
- *Rate card for products for different credit periods.*
- *All incentives to Chiranjib was linked to price discounting levels.*

Also, his manager made a conscious effort to go with Chiranjib to few key customers and show how to firmly yet politely negotiate with customers.

Following the principles, Chiranjib then became a Champion Sales Person!

*****

DNA 9–Ready Reckoner – Negotiation Skills

Preventive Negotiations
1. *Negotiating* to meet the *right* person.
2. *Negotiating* to meet the *right* person at the customer place at the right time.
3. *Negotiating* to meet the *right* person at the right time at the right place.
4. *Negotiating* and *agreeing* on the *right* product and solution.
5. *Negotiating* a *confirmation* from the customer that the product you have quoted is right.
6. *Negotiating* a *confirmation* from the customer that there is no issue with your brand.
7. *Negotiating* a *confirmation* from the customer that there is no issue with your service support.

Every Small Thing Matters (ESTM) Negotiations
1. Break down the product / solution / service you are selling into as many small things (variables) as possible
2. Put a price/value for every little thing (every variable)
3. Negotiate with the customer for every small thing (every variable).
4. What is small to you may be big to customer. What is small to the customer may be is big to you.

Give Value Not Discount (GVND) Negotiations
1. Matching customer price should be the last option.
2. Instead of price discount, give or show additional value in return.
3. Worst case, meet customer midway by giving 50% of what he is asking as price discount and balance 50% as value.

Long Term Lock-up (LTL) Negotiations
1. Sign-up long term price agreement or rate contracts or schemes. 2. Expand the revenue scope of your business by negotiating a commitment from the customer for either higher volume or longer period price validity or higher share of wallet etc. 3. Give targets to customers and link to rewards – wherein the customer gets to earn significant benefits when they give you business beyond a specific volume or revenue.

Let us never negotiate out of fear. But let us never fear to negotiate

~ John F Kennedy

They said the same thing, but in very different ways.

Notes

SALES STORY 10.1

What is a real success?

Department of Telecom had floated a large RFP (Request for Proposal) for the project of up-gradation of existing old telecom equipment. It was one of the largest and most prestigious telecom projects in the country. Several national and multinational companies were willing to participate in the project.Abhishek who was working as a business manager in an MNC *ZeeTech*, one of the pioneers in the telecom industry was also one of the front runners in this deal. Abhishek was an old hat in the telecom industry and has worked in a couple of other telecom companies before joining *ZeeTech*. One of such company was *TisTel.* Rupesh, who was the business manager at *TisTel* was on old friend of Abhishek. Both Abhishek and Rupesh had started their career together.

During a weekend party, over a glass of beer, Rupesh asked Abhishek, "Bro how are you guys preparing for the upcoming tender submission for the mega-deal at the Department of Telecom."

"Oh Man, Can't tell you how crazy this has been last few days in office. The whole company seems to be only working on this deal nowadays. I can tell you one thing, with so many testing, benchmarking and approvals to be completed, tonnes of papers to be signed, what with so much of legal and financial implications, these mega deals are soul-sucking" replied Abhishek gulping his beer.

"How are you guys preparing, I am sure things won't be different in *TisTel* as well," asked Abhishek."They are indeed maddening" replied Rupesh. After a brief pause, Rupesh continued

"Bro, I have an offer for you."

"What's that" asked Abhishek.

"You know this is a life-changing bid for everyone, If you let us win, by telling us the prices that you guys will be quoting, I can arrange for money much more than the sales incentive that you will get after winning this deal" Rupesh looked straight at Abhishek

Abhishek didn't reply. His eyebrows twitched. Rupesh knew his friend was in a dilemma. He continued, "Bro, this will be a WIN-WIN for both of us, I get the incentive from the company for winning the deal, and you also get paid for losing. Both will get rich. After all, why the hell we work for? We work for money, right? *ZeeTech* is big enough a company and losing one multimillion deal will not make any dents to their overall business. But look at us we are mere pawns in this big game. Working like slaves for these big companies, we need to help each other, help each other to earn as much money as we can. Irrespective of whichever company wins or loses, both of us will win and make our lives better."

Abhishek kept on looking at his friend. His words were making his head spin.

Mulling Exercise:

1. *What do you think Abhishek should do now?*
2. *Was Rupesh right in doing what he did?*
3. *What would you have done in this situation?*

Sales Story 10.2

Under the table

Sameer was the Distribution account manager in charge of a sizeable distributor for a strong consumer brand for Delhi NCR. This distributor was one of the three distributors operating in that geography. While profit margins in this distribution business were wafer-thin, however, the crux of the business lay in fast *rotation* of inventory. More rapid rotation meant making the product available off the shelf as soon as the demand emerges and immediately backfilling the list. So faster the revenue was generated better the profitability of the overall business. Which meant achieving all the sales targets and buying smartly would ensure distributor would end up making reasonable margins.

This fast rotation bought along with it *added sales pressure*, which meant giving commitments and support to retailers who would buy from the distributor for the sell-out of the material from their stock and also providing more credit period than what was required in few cases.

Such tactics brought with it a definite risk of cash flow issues from time to time, along with the erosion of margins. Picking up the right models to stock in right quantity at right time was essential to achieving both top-line and bottom-line.

During one of the quarter ends, Sameer and the distribution company's CEO Vishal had their drink to unwind after a high-pressure quarter end. Vishal asked Sameer

"I have a proposal for you…If you support me, we can grow this business profitably and with less pressure."

"What is it, Vishal Ji?" Sameer's eyes twinkled.

"Well, why don't you help me get some of the inventory at special prices. These could be special models, which are going to be the end of life soon or models where you want me to pick up entire stock so that no other distributor is carrying that model with them" replied Vishal

"How will it help you?"

"Well, if you can somehow get me the inventory at 5% less compared to other distributors, I will pass this saving to some of the key retailers and tie up my volumes and…

"And…?" Sameer was getting hooked.

"I will give you 1% on my sales…Why don't you go for the US holiday with your wife that you always wanted to go…I will sponsor it?" Replied Vishal sipping the last of the drink from his glass.

"Well………" thoughts were wrestling inside Sameer's bald head….

Mulling Exercise:

1. *What should Sameer do?*
2. *What will happen if he takes the offer from Vishal?*
3. *Was Vishal right in tempting Sameer with a US holiday*

****

Sales Story 10.3

Travelling to unknown places

Adarsh was filling up the monthly expense sheet that needed to be submitted by 10th of every month. His company allowed him to claim local conveyance reimbursement at the rate of Rs. 10 per KM in case the salespersons use their own vehicles or taxi fare at actuals.

Adarsh had made about 20 calls that month using his own car, and his expenses were roughly coming to Rs. 8000 for the month. However, Adarsh made an expense claim for 30 calls and claimed Rs. 12000 by faking entries for additional 10 sales calls. By doing this he made cool Rs. 4000 extra. He has seen his senior colleagues do this so he also over claimed without any worry...Infact, he has been doing that for over a year....

One day a finance manager who cleared the claims made an observation to his CFO.

"Sir, last month, the Zonal Head had a full day review on the 15th....I know it because he had called me for the AR report which I made and sent to him." Said the Finance Manager

"So?" asked the CFO (Chief Financial Officer)

"I was checking the local claim submitted and saw that one of the salespersons has claimed for conveyance on

15th for two sales calls. I was just wondering?.........." the finance manager couldn't complete the sentence as the CFO intervened in between.

"Are you saying he has fudged....this is serious..." The CFO asked angrily.

"Sir, I also went back and checked that sales guy's claims for previous months...there are standard same customer calls and those customers don't even appear in the funnel regularly" replied the finance manager.

"OK..get me the details...let me have a chat with the Zonal Head.." said the CFO.

"OK, Sir..."

Mulling Exercise:

1. *What do you think happened next?*
2. *Should Adarsh have fudged his expense report?*
3. *When his seniors and colleagues are also doing the same thing, what is wrong in Adarsh doing?*
4. *Should Adarsh's manager be checking the reports proactively to ensure these kinds of things don't become a habit?*

Sales Story 10.4

Honey, it's all about money

Mahesh was a salesperson in an instrumentation company that sold mainly to industries, research laboratories and educational institutions. Most of the business happens on special pricing and is done through value-added resellers (VARs) who manage these customer accounts by handling the relationships, transaction, payments etc.

While Mahesh worked with 5 different VARs in his territory, his favourite was Macrotech Instruments. He would do 40% of his business through this partner. He had an intimate understanding with the owner of Macrotech. The agreement was, Mahesh would ensure a 10% margin for Macrotech in every deal, and anything above 10% needs to be passed on to him at a personal level. He would ensure he sold to end customer at a reasonable price, get special price clearance from his company and pocket anything above 10% dealer margin. Macrotech would give this money as cash to Mahesh so that there is no transaction trail or proof. Even better, he would slip it into envelopes during birthday parties and anniversary dinners organized by Mahesh in the pretext of a gift.

After a few years, Mahesh got transferred from Delhi to Mumbai. In his place, Ramesh took over his customer accounts. Few months down the road, as he started handling transactions, he realized that customers were buying at reasonable prices but, Macrotech was always pushing him for special price clearances. Ramesh began pushing back and started clearing higher rates. The CEO of Macrotech one day called Ramesh for dinner and approached him with similar arrangement as the one he was having with Mahesh. Ramesh was shocked when he heard the proposal from Macrotech.

Mulling Exercise:

1. *What did Ramesh do next?*
2. *Was Mahesh right in doing what he did? After all, he ensured his company business did not suffer.*

*****

DNA Number 10: ETHICAL – DOES NOT COMPROMISE ON PERSONAL AND ORGANIZATION VALUES

What do you mean by Ethics?

It is being true to yourself and your values. It is ensuring you do not break law. It is ensuring you abide by the rules of the organization you work for. It is ensuring you comply with the provisions of society you live in. It is ensuring you do not cross the lines of decency. It is ensuring you do not harm or sabotage another human being's efforts knowingly.

There are five stakeholders you are committed to when it comes to being ethical:

1. **Yourself** – Being true to yourself.
2. **Your family** – Being true to your family.
3. **Your society** – Being true to the place you reside.
4. **Your employer** – Being true to your employer and employer values.
5. **Your Customer**–Being true to your customer and their values.

Being true to yourself:

First and foremost for being ethical is being true to oneself. We had all heard from our parents, this famous proverb when we were growing up. "When wealth is lost nothing is lost. When health is lost something is lost. When character is lost, everything is lost." It is essential that we grow specific values, like, being honest, sincere, truthful, kind and humble and ensure they stay with us all our lives. We could write an entire book on the virtues of the values mentioned above, but in the scope of the present topic in this book, we would limit ourselves to only highlighting the readers about these seemingly basic but very important values that one should inculcate in life.

We should remember that money is a by-product and no end goal. If we make money as our end goal at any cost then in the pursuit of this goal our actions will lead us to commit one mistake after the other which can end up ruining our personal as well as professional life. Real success is what you earn using right practices.

Being true to your family:

Without your family's support, you can never grow in your professional career. It is essential to identify the fact that they are your co-pilot and ensure you are transparent to them. If you start neglecting your work because of family compulsions and vice versa, if you start neglecting your family because of work compulsions, you will never be successful in both. If you are transparent with your family on the kind of work you do, you will find a lot of support which will help you perform your job without worry.

Being true to your society:

It is important to be a good citizen and abide by the laws of the land you are residing and working. This means paying taxes correctly and on time, not committing any crimes however minor they may be! If you are careless, these mistakes will come to haunt you later in your career. Nowadays, large and reputed companies do background verification of employees before they hire them. You may lose out on opportunity to work with a reputed company at a bigger salary if they find out that you have had legal issues which you are hiding.

Being true to your employer:

It is ensuring you don't violate your company's rules and regulations. It is ensuring you adhere to your company policies. Your violating company rules and procedures may lead to loss of customers, revenue, profits and reputation for your company. It may lead to even your termination, which will impact your reputation and career.

Being true to your customer:

You need to ensure your customers are not cheated, taken for a ride. You need to ensure all the commitments you gave customer are met, and you need to ensure you only commit deliverables that are within the capabilities of your company and business partner.

Just to summarise, what happens when you violate ethics:

1. You run the risk of facing legal action and even going to jail.
2. You run the risk of losing your job and career. With bad references, nobody else will give you a job.
3. You run the risk of losing your reputation and that of your family.
4. You run the risk of losing your peace of mind and ability to sleep fitfully.
5. Your company runs the risk of losing customers, revenues, margins and reputation because of you.
6. Your company runs of the risk of facing legal action because of you and paying huge fines and settlements to governments and customers.
7. Your colleagues run the risk of losing their jobs and careers.
8. Your customers run the risk of losing productivity and business.
9. There are people in customer organizations who interacted with you, who could face the loss of jobs, careers and reputations.

10. Your dealers, resellers, business partners may end up facing severe consequences.
11. Your dealers, resellers, business partners may end up shutting down their businesses.

There are many examples in the world today of people losing their entire life's work and ruining their reputations forever. Take the examples of leading cricketers, top bank CEOs who were once awarded and rewarded, but now facing a ruined life.

Let us see what happened in each of the sales stories above…

Sales Story 10.1….

Abhishek agreed to Rupesh's deal and leaked price information. Rupesh's company was about to quote an even lower price because they really needed this business and because of Rupesh's insistence and confidence (because he had Abhishek's price information) they quoted slightly higher with the surety that the deal is theirs. But in a shocking twist, a third competitor quoted lower and picked up the whole deal. Infact if Rupesh had gone with the price initially approved by his company, he would have easily won the deal. Because of his wrong reading of the situation and mistaken understanding of which competition was stronger or weaker, he ended up losing the deal for his company. Subsequently Rupesh got fired.

Sales Story 10.2….

Sameer's deal with distributor flourished for over a year. He made fancy foreign trips with his family and even booked a bigger house. But one day, in a drunken stupor, the distribution CEO blurted out their arrangement to someone known to Sameer's boss, and the news leaked. Subsequently Sameer was let go. He joined a new company where he started similar arrangement with the same distributor because by now he was used to his expensive lifestyle. However, he ended up losing this job also, and because of his reputation he never got another job. He started a business in completely different industry because he could not interact with his old colleagues and associates any more.

The distributor also by now had acquired a lousy reputation, and all brands who were doing business with the distributor started behaving very cautiously. Slowly the distributor mended his ways but could never be the top distributor for any of the brand he was associated with.

Sales Story 10.3….

Adarsh was confronted by the CFO and his manager, and he did not have any plausible explanation. He was asked to resign. He resigned and joined another company at similar levels and had to work for another few years at the same level before he could get promoted. His career growth speed reduced.

Sales Story 10.4….

Ramesh without wasting any time went and complained to his manager about Macrotech and his offer. His manager confronted Macrotech, and they came to know about Mahesh. Mahesh was dismissed from service. Also Macrotech was removed as a dealer. Ramesh was complimented for his honesty and promoted soon. He rebuilt all the relationships with this customers and got another dealer to take care of all the requirements. Today Ramesh is head of a large sales organization and is doing very well.

*****

DNA 10–Self-Exercise by Mr./Ms:____________

My Ethics Code:

Please write down your personal ethics code/goals that you want to follow in your life

S.No	Ethics Code
1	
2	
3	
4	
5	
6	
7	
8	
9	
10	

*****

Notes

Way Forward–Remaining A Champion for Ever

Let's first summarize the Ten DNA's of a Champion Sales Person

C	CONFIDENT: HAVING THE WILL TO WIN
H	HONORS COMMITMENTS: "SAY WHAT YOU DO AND DO WHAT YOU SAY"
R	RIGOR IN EXECUTION–HAS A PLAN AND A BACK-UP PLAN
O	OWNERSHIP OF FAILURE–NO EGO, NO BUCK PASSING, A TEAM PLAYER
M	MAPS CUSTOMER THOROUGHLY – HAS A CLEAR RELATIONSHIP STRATEGY
O	OBSERVER AND A LISTENER – ABILITY TO UNDERSTAND CUSTOMER NEEDS
S	SOLID PRODUCT KNOWLEDGE – KNOWS WHAT TO SELL AND HOW TO SELL
O	ORATOR – ABILITY TO COMMUNICATE EFFECTIVELY IN DIFFERENT FORUMS
M	MASTER NEGOTIATOR – ENSURES WIN-WIN FOR BOTH CUSTOMER AND THE ORGANIZATION
E	ETHICAL – DOES NOT COMPROMISE ON PERSONAL AND ORGANIZATION VALUES

****

Lets look at the first four DNAs:

C	CONFIDENT: HAVING THE WILL TO WIN
H	HONORS COMMITMENTS: "SAY WHAT YOU DO AND DO WHAT YOU SAY"
R	RIGOR IN EXECUTION–HAS A PLAN AND A BACK-UP PLAN
O	OWNERSHIP OF FAILURE–NO EGO, NO BUCK PASSING, A TEAM PLAYER

The above four DNAs can be classified under two behavior characteristics:

ATTITUDE

DISCIPLINE

The Champion Sales persons have a great positive attitude, are extremely disciplined in their personal and work life and therefore they are always confident, extremely trustworthy, ever dependable and will leave no stone unturned to achieve their's and their team's goals.

******

Lets look at the next six DNAs:

M	MAPS CUSTOMER THOROUGHLY – HAS A CLEAR RELATIONSHIP STRATEGY
O	OBSERVER AND A LISTENER – ABILITY TO UNDERSTAND CUSTOMER NEEDS
S	SOLID PRODUCT KNOWLEDGE – KNOWS WHAT TO SELL AND HOW TO SELL
O	ORATOR – ABILITY TO COMMUNICATE EFFECTIVELY IN DIFFERENT FORUMS
M	MASTER NEGOTIATOR – ENSURES WIN-WIN FOR BOTH CUSTOMER AND THE ORGANIZATION
E	ETHICAL – DOES NOT COMPROMISE ON PERSONAL AND ORGANIZATION VALUES

The above six DNAs can be classified under three behavior characteristics:

ATTENTION TO DETAIL

+

PREPARATION

+

TENACITY

The Champion Sales persons are able to breakdown their tasks into small, manageable details, are well prepared for any customer situation and they never give up

******

To ensure you always remain a Champion through¬out your career, you need to:

A	ATTITUDE
D	DISCIPLINE
A	ATTENTION TO DETAIL
P	PREPARATION
T	TENACITY

Champions ADAPT.

Change is inevitable....You will change company, you will change industry, you will change your city of work, you will become a manager, you will start your business, you will go through ups and downs

Only way you will remain a champion is to ADAPT. Adapt to the new city, new company, new rules and policies, new products and technologies, new ways of working, new customers, new government regulations and laws and help groom up freshers and juniors in your team by being patient and teaching them all that you know...

Remember, Change is the only constant. The person who adapts to these changes fast and yet retains his CHAMPION CHROMOSOME will always emerge the winner.

******

What are CEOs saying about Champion Sales Persons

Mr. Ravi Swaminathan,

Formerly Managing Director of AMD India, Formerly Vice President and MD of Hewlett Packard India.

The first thing I look for in a sales person is hunger-the internal driving force to achieve and exceed on one's commitments, the tenacity to hang in there when things are tough, the ability to close a sale and get the order in.

The second key quality is the ability to build strong inter-person relationships both internally within the organisation, and externally with the customer, across multiple levels. The salesman must be able to talk to the CEO and to the "peon" in the government office , without being over-awed in one case or patronising in the other instance. Relationships are built on trust, and the salesman must build his credibility, by consistently delivering on his promise and responding quickly and transparently to customer issues.

The third key strength is one's shrewdness, the ability to size up a situation, understand the relationship dynamics, what are the unspoken needs of the buyer, and an understanding of what one needs to bring to the table to succeed.

All these qualities have to be underpinned with a high degree of personal integrity. Without integrity, and with the above three qualities, the rep is a ticking time bomb.

My only input to an aspiring sales person is " Be yourself". First understand yourself, and recognise that there are multiple styles for being a successful sales person. Understand in what situations you are at your best-in cracking new businesses, in building on existing relationships, with channels, or with a few deep OEM relationships. Finally ,do you enjoy being a sales person? It is a tough and demanding job, if you don't enjoy it , look at something else to do. Often, we can get trapped in a job where we are miserable, and very early in your career, you should find out your best fit.

There is one case which still resonates with me, and which I encountered very early in my career. I had two salesman, one was smart, well-dressed and a great communicator. He had an aura of confidence, which made you believe that he was great in everything he did. The other salesman was poorly dressed, had an effeminate voice, and "zero" personality. When I took over the region, I wondered how he had ever been selected, and was not sure how long he would last.

Yet, when I watched them in action over the next one year and looked at their performance, I slowly was forced to realise that the effeminate, zero personality sales rep had the best record. He was unassuming, but the buyers liked that, and he would disarm them to get what he wanted. On the other hand, the hot-shot guy turned out to be an ace bull-sh.......and more dangerously, could not be trusted. He was a consummate politician .

That is when I realised that personal interviews very rarely help you select the right candidate. In the 15-20 minutes you talk to the candidate, the smart communicator invariably wins out, not the silent performer. Ideally, I look at the track record(even though that can be manipulated at times), and more importantly references from people whose assessment you respect.

****

Mr. Rajiv Srivastava,

Managing Director & CEO of Indian Energy Exchange, Formerly COO of Hewlett Packard Asia Pacific and Japan.

I was just twiddling my thumbs lazily on an extremely chilly, blistery morning within the first fortnight of my initiation as a sales person. Not having a clue regarding how to go about organising my work, I mustered enough courage to seek out my boss.

Pat came her response "Go out, make cold calls and give me an update end of day of your activities."

The simplicity of her words hit me hard – and almost 30 years later to this day, that remains one of the most profound sales coaching I have ever received. All selling happens when you meet the customer and unless you engage with one there can never be any outcome. Just showing up is such a big part of the battle won.

Early in my sales career there were times when I was under observation. Nervous but confident that I would not disappoint myself. That's not how it turned out and my boss said I was sailing by – enough to survive, not good enough to achieve the success I so desired. It struck me to the core. I wanted to be so great to put competition to shame

That honest conversation made me self-reflect. I became a constant student of what it takes for a sales person to succeed. A lot has changed in sales over the years – what customers buy and how, their expectations, medium of communication shifting between physical to digital, how you reach out to solicit, content in messages, tactics, measures of success. However a few traits continue to be defining for a standout performance and let me elaborate.

The best sales persons own everything. The phrase that I often use with sales teams is that either you have reasons or you have results. The people who give reasons do not produce results and those with results have no need to give reasons – they simply make things happen. It is not as if they have it easier. We all have our starting points and the most significant difference between perennial top performers and everyone else is attitude. Elite sales people approach their job with a mindset that they own the organisation, that everything happening around them is controlled by them and they are accountable. Power lies within and not externally and that internal locus of control correlates with success at work, higher income and better index of happiness. No coincidence that the same people make it to the leader board year after year.

Regardless of what you are selling – product, service or advice – people buy based on feelings. And establishing that emotional connect perhaps gets the best outcomes. Had a very interesting conversation with a customer on a Sunday afternoon. The Managing Director of a large engineering organisation called to inform that their order was getting delayed and politely enquiring if it will impact the sales person. No better way of ensuring your success than getting the customer to have a stake in your career progression. People have confidence in you and believe they can depend on you – that you mean what you say and will do as such.

While it would be perfectly in order to think of many more qualities that make for a successful sales career, let me round up by saying that character is everything. Guard your integrity as a sacred thing–in business and sales success you must have credibility. Element of trust is often the distinguishing factor between one salesperson and another and between companies.

A career in sales is challenging as well as rewarding, clearly not for the faint hearted. Just one look at the who's who of the corporate world would make it apparent that many of the senior leaders and chief executives had started their professional life in sales. This gains even more significance and relevance in today's dynamic environment. Organisations have to reinvent themselves to lead basis customer and other external feedback. Who better to manage that transformation than sales with a 360 view!

****

MR. A V SATEESH KUMAR,

Former Managing Director of D.Light, Former Executive Vice President – Operations at SKS Micro finance, Former President – Insurance at India Infoline.

A smiling nature with a positive attitude is one of the main tenets of a successful sales person. While Sales is pervasive in every part of our life – we sell our ideas to our family, competencies to our employer, love to our partner, loyalty to our country etc, it is one profession which is mis-understood and looked at negatively by everyone. If someone is selling any product or idea to you, it is assumed that he / she is interested in their own benefit and are trying to rip you off ! With this background, it is important for the sales person to come across with honesty and has to convince the customer that the product/service/idea being offered is for their benefit. One should not be in a hurry else the customer may start doubting the intentions.

Sales is one profession which is very rewarding in many ways. One can get instant gratification through incentives and contests, recognition through promotions and even raise to the CEO position. As Sales contribute to both the top and bottom line of company, Sales managers are the most sought after by the top management. While Sales team can enjoy all the attention and incentives, they also are on the firing line when things do not go well.

Champion sales people have most of these qualities ie Discipline, hardworking, planning, pleasant attitude, perseverance and street smartness. I had the good fortune of working with some of the sales people who had all of these qualities and were immensely successful. Watching them on a sales call is a pleasure – they initially probe the customer to understand their need, suggest appropriate product, nudge the customer to take the right decision and then close the sale making everyone happy. At no time, they display hurry or eagerness to conclude the sale. These sales people are genuinely interested in the benefit of the customer as they are not just making a sale but building long term relationships. I have noticed that these sales people get multiple sales or qualified referred leads from these satisfied customers.

It is a common assumption that sales is an easy job and one just needs to be glib talker and cunning to fool the customer. Truth cannot be farther than that. Sales is an art which needs to be mastered over many years through practice, learning from others and reading about great sales people. Satisfied customers are your best brand ambassadors and hence great sales people look at long term success rather than short term gains.

****

Notes

About Author

Raghuraman

Raghuraman is a leading sales trainer and a sales process consultant, with more than 25 years of sales and marketing experience. He has lead large sales teams during his stints as a senior leader in large organizations like Hewlett Packard India and AMD India. In 2012, he started his own sales training company, Salezart Consulting (www.salezart.com), which has trained and motivated more than fifteen thousand sales professionals across different segments and verticals in different disciplines, over the last seven years. He has also launched an exclusive app for sales professionals, which is probably the only LMS in India exclusively designed for sales professionals. Currently the "SALEZART" LMS app has thousands of sales persons improving their selling skills online 24X7. He loves music and constantly listens to old Hindi songs and Ilayaraja's Tamil and Telugu songs on a daily basis. He is also a voracious reader of good books. He is married to Uma, a leading food blogger, and has two children. He is based out of Gurgaon, Delhi NCR.

Tanmay Dubey

Tanmay Dubey, is the best selling author of 'JUST SIX EVENINGS' (2015) 'THE AMIGOS' (2017) 'THE RED LINE' (2019). He finds solace in long distance running and has actively participated in many national and international Marathons. He is also an avid cyclist and has successfully completed IRON MAN Australia Triathlon.

Tanmay has a professional experience of over 20 years working in leadership roles for companies like DELL Technologies, Oracle and Hewlett-Packard.

Tanmay lives in Gurgaon with his Wife and Daughter. He can be reached at Twitter (@Author_Tanmay), Instagram on @thetanmaydubey and Facebook on his Page